UNEXPLAINED
ZODIAC

The Inside Story to Your Sign

Sasha Fenton

imagine!
Publishing

For Charles Nurnberg

An Imagine Book
Published by Charlesbridge Publishing, Inc.
85 Main Street, Watertown, MA 02472
(617) 926-0329
www.charlesbridge.com

Library of Congress Cataloging-in-Publication Data
Fenton, Sasha.
 Unexplained zodiac: the inside story to your sign / Sasha Fenton.
   pages cm
ISBN 978-1-62354-003-6
1. Zodiac. 2. Astrology. I. Title.
BF1726.F465 2012
133.5'2--dc23
                          2012044150

2 4 6 8 10 9 7 5 3 1

For information about custom editions, special sales,
premium and corporate purchases, please contact
Charlesbridge Publishing at specialsales@charlesbridge.com

TABLE OF CONTENTS

Introduction: The Inside Story..1

1. The Unexplained Zodiac...4

2. Astrology Factoids..8

3. About the Zodiac..13

4. Sideways Astrology 19

5. Reflected Astrology 23

6. Astro-Compatibility...26

7. Virtues and Vices...42

8. Sun Sign Aries...47

9. Sun Sign Taurus..56

10. Sun Sign Gemini... **65**

11. Sun Sign Cancer **74**

12. Sun Sign Leo **83**

13. Sun Sign Virgo **92**

14. Sun Sign Libra.. **101**

15. Sun Sign Scorpio..**110**

16. Sun Sign Sagittarius...**118**

17. Sun Sign Capricorn **127**

18. Sun Sign Aquarius **135**

19. Sun Sign Pisces.. **145**

    Conclusion: Beyond the Sun Sign...................................... **153**

INTRODUCTION:
THE INSIDE STORY

It makes sense for an inside story to come from an insider, and as far as checking out real people in light of their Sun signs, that has to be me—if for no other reason than the sheer length of time I've spent working in the field. Also, this introduction shows my own personal "inside story."

In the late 1960s and early 1970s, I became fascinated with astrology, especially psychological astrology, but in those days, it was hard to locate information.

At that time, I worked as a secretary to a pleasant man in his late sixties, and when he heard of my interest in astrology, he tried to help. He gave me the phone number of a friend of his who worked as an herbalist and astrologer, and suggested that I call the man and ask him for advice. I rang the number and found myself talking to a bad-tempered old guy who had no intention whatsoever of helping me, but— presumably because I was connected to his friend—he deigned to give me a piece of advice. He asked if I knew how to erect an astrological chart. It wasn't a silly question, because in those pre-computer days, horoscope charts involved a good deal of hand calculations. On hearing that I could cope with the technical stuff, the grumpy man advised me to do *five hundred charts* free of charge for total strangers, and that way, I would end up knowing my job!

That advice would have finished most people, but if he'd taken a look at my horoscope he'd have seen that I have massive amounts of patience for those things that I consider worth doing. I followed his advice to the letter and discovered that he was right. In effect, the road I was forced to take meant that I learned my craft in a totally hands-on way, by doing charts, talking to clients, and spotting patterns in personality, behavior, and lifestyle. In the meantime, I read everything I could get my hands on about psychology, and when decent astrology books started to come to the UK market, I read all those as well.

In time, I obtained full qualifications as an astrologer, and I also spent many years serving on prestigious astrological committees. The longer I worked in the field, the more I questioned the established views on Sun sign astrology, and it struck me that there was a considerable gap between the "received wisdom" that was copied from one astrology book to the next and the reality of the clients who I dealt with on a daily basis. I realized that most people *are* like their Sun signs to an extent, but that the Sun sign information itself doesn't match up to reality. In time, I built up a mental body of knowledge, some of which matched standard astrological opinion and some did not—and that's what you'll see in this book.

The only real people who appear in this book are several wonderful friends whom I have used to illustrate the best aspects of their respective Sun signs. Other than these individuals, the personalities described in the book are amalgams of groups of people. I've blended and combined their stories to show the true natures of the Sun signs, and to bring them to life in a way that lengthy descriptions cannot do.

I have pointed out the unexpected niceness of those signs that suffer from bad press and the unexpected hardness of those that are often described as soft and sweet, along with the particular small faults of all of the signs. Get ready for the inside story, as that will help you to understand the bizarre nature of the Sun signs and the ways you and I fit within them.

CHAPTER ONE:
THE UNEXPLAINED ZODIAC

The bizarre thing about astrology is that it *works*, and nobody can fully explain *why* it works!

Astrologers come from every walk of life, some of them top-class scientists and mathematicians, yet none have been able to come up with a valid explanation. Many highly intelligent skeptics have decided to take a look at astrology in order to prove that it is nothing more than superstition, and in many cases end up becoming astrologers themselves! For instance, in the mid-1950s, two French psychologists, Michel Gauquelin and his wife, Françoise Schneider-Gauquelin, set out by means of statistical studies to prove whether astrology could possibly work. Their work showed that the position of the planets at birth *did* in fact lay down the basis of character, aptitudes, and destiny.

There is a world of difference between the astrology of newspaper columns and *real* astrology, which requires a full birth chart and an astrologer who knows how to interpret it. I'm sure everyone is aware of this by now. However, the Sun sign is the only piece that we all know from our date of birth alone, so this book can only focus on the inside story of the Sun signs.

If you have no idea of your Sun sign, you can look it up right here. The precise dates for the Sun signs alter slightly from year to year, so if you were born on the cusp of two signs (on the days at the very beginning or very end of a sign's range), please consult an astrologer, as he or she will be able to tell you your Sun sign in a matter of minutes. In the meantime, here are the average dates:

Average Sun Sign Dates

SIGN	DATES
Aries	March 21–April 19
Taurus	April 20–May 20
Gemini	May 21–June 21
Cancer	June 22–July 22
Leo	July 23–August 22
Virgo	August 23–September 22
Libra	September 23–October 22

Scorpio	October 23–November 21
Sagittarius	November 22–December 21
Capricorn	December 22–January 20
Aquarius	January 21–February 18
Pisces	February 19–March 20

It should also be clear that a book of this kind can only reflect generalities for a subject as involved as astrology. Please keep in mind that you may not entirely fit the descriptions within, because your Moon sign, Rising sign, planets, houses, and much more will have an effect on your personality and your life. Even two people born on the same day will have some differences—although they will also have many similarities.

THE WEIRD EFFECT ASTROLOGY HAS ON SOME PEOPLE

Some people think there are weak-minded folk who can hardly take a breath without consulting an astrologer, but after forty years in the field, I haven't met any of them. If people get into astrology to any extent, they inevitably end up studying it for themselves, and then it slips into being an occasional pleasure rather than a daily obsession. Fortunately, astrology is easy to learn, and nowadays there's plenty of inexpensive software that takes the pain out of chart calculation.

The strangest effect isn't people taking it too seriously; it's the incandescent rage that descends upon certain otherwise clever folk when it comes to our subject. A favorite criticism, among those who presumably have a high IQ or at least some *astronomical* knowledge, is that the constellations have moved over the last two centuries and that the signs are no longer where astrologers say they are. This phenomenon is called the precession of the equinoxes, and it's caused by the slight wobble in the spin of the Earth, which makes the world move backward against the backdrop of the zodiac over time. Needless to say, this phenomenon is well known to astrologers, and has been for the past ten millennia.

Western astrologers use the tropical zodiac, which could be called seasonal astrology, because it links the signs of the zodiac to the equinoxes and the solstices. Hindu or Vedic astrologers use the sidereal zodiac, which links astrology to the current position of the constellations that takes account of the precession of the equinoxes. They use astrology in a different way than we do, but their systems work for them, and that's what matters.

Sometimes astronomers tell us that there are actually *thirteen* signs of the zodiac. They suddenly decide that we should include Ophiuchus, or perhaps Arachne, in the zodiac. As it happens, we are perfectly well aware that there are actually *forty-eight* constellations that are close by or touching the belt of the zodiac, including Ophiuchus the Snake, Arachne the Spider, Cetus the Whale, and many others.

Many astrologers are also into astronomy. Some astronomers are brave enough to study astrology as well, but they consider it necessary to do so in secret. How ridiculous is that? I am certain that one day in the not-too-distant future, a full scientific explanation for astrology *will* emerge, and then, hopefully, the criticism will stop.

In the meantime, let us look at how the Sun signs affect us.

CHAPTER TWO:
ASTROLOGY FACTOIDS

- Every civilization on Earth has developed some form of astrology, but it worked a little too well for the comfort of some rulers, so it often ended up being banned.

- The first writings about astrology are among the first writings about anything. The first real town may have been Ur in Chaldea, in what is now southern Iraq. Chaldean priests studied and wrote about astrology, although at that time, and for a long time afterward, it was lumped in with astronomy and the beginnings of science in general, along with the need to invent a workable calendar for planting, harvesting, hunting, fishing, and propitiating the gods.

- Astrology spread out from Mesopotamia to China, India, and Europe, where local mythology and beliefs became entwined within it.

- Various kings banned astrology in China, but they allowed Buddhist monks to study numerology. So the monks made codes out of their astrological knowledge, and eventually the original astrological roots became lost and forgotten.

- Without astrology, there would have been no astronomical data and very little knowledge of physics and science. Even as astrology was being pushed aside, many great minds still used it. For example, Isaac Newton, Tycho Brahe, Johannes Kepler, Nicolaus Copernicus, and Carl Jung.

- There are many references to astrology in the bible, some merely a note of the times of new moons and planets as a clock or a calendar.

- Chaucer and Shakespeare often used astrology in their work.

- The most popular websites for Internet surfers are those devoted to astrology.

- One website has concluded that 75 percent of those who read astrology columns are women. Looking back to the years when I was a consultant astrologer, I'd say that's probably about right. Men tend to consult astrologers when their lives are in turmoil. Women do this as well, but they also like to have a reading every now and then just to keep an eye on the way things are going and to see if there is anything interesting on the horizon.

- About one third of people in the United States believe in astrology; it's probably more in parts of Europe. Other than in Muslim communities, many Asian cultures are into astrology, although in many cases it's Chinese astrology rather than our Western version.

- Nancy Reagan consulted an astrologer after her husband was shot, and she's not alone. Princess Diana of England consulted psychics, and many other political figures (including Kate Middleton, the new Duchess of Cambridge) have done so on at least one occasion.

- Many business executives consult astrologers on a fairly regular basis, though they won't necessarily admit to it. Actually, many business executives are very intuitive and even psychic, so that makes them even more open to such things as astrology.

- Stock traders definitely use astrology, and they tend to be open about it. I did the daily horoscopes for Michael Bloomberg's organization in London for a couple of years—and it was Mr. Bloomberg himself who interviewed me for the job and took me on.

- Adolf Hitler used an astrologer, but sent him to die in a concentration camp when he started reporting that things would not continue to go his way. (Long before Hitler came into power, an astrologer named Elspeth Ebertin predicted that he would become Führer.)

- Nostradamus is said to have predicted World War II, the assassination of President Kennedy, and the attack on the World Trade Center's Twin Towers in New York City.

- In the United Kingdom and the United States, you can now obtain recognized university qualifications and even a doctorate in astrology, often linked with culture, religion, astronomy, and history.

- There are many branches of astrology. For instance, astro-cartography and local space astrology are both astrology of place rather than time. These systems are useful if you intend to travel or live in another location.

- Local space feng shui astrology shows how you can make the best use of your home for luck and happiness, and it isn't hard to do yourself.

ASTROLOGY/ASTRONOMY WORDS IN GENERAL USE

- **consider**: this means "with the stars" —e.g., look at the stars before taking action

- **disaster**: this supposes that the stars are causing a serious problem

- **influenza**: this word means "a bad influence"

- **jovial**: this means being jolly, as the god, Jupiter, supposedly was

- **lunatic**: supposedly someone who loses their mind when the Moon is full

- **martial**: a military person who is supposedly like the god, Mars

- **mazel tov**: amazingly, this means "may the stars be in a good alignment for you today"

- **mercurial**: this implies that someone is quick to think and act, like Mercury

- **saturnine**: indicating someone who is serious and dour, like Saturn

- **venereal disease**: supposedly a disease of Venus resulting from sexual activity

CHAPTER THREE:
ABOUT THE ZODIAC

The zodiac is a belt of stars that appears to move around the central part of the Earth. In ancient times, astronomers and astrologers thought the Sun orbited the Earth and that it traveled through the constellations of the zodiac while doing so. By 1609, astronomers had discovered that the Sun was in the center of the system and that the Earth was just one of the planets that orbited it, and the reason why planets sometimes appeared to go backward through the sky.

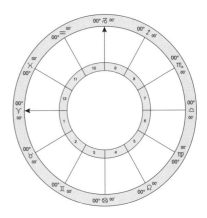

When you read the stars columns in magazines, you will see comments such as *This is an earth sign* or *This is a fixed sign.* The following will show you the complete pattern.

THE PATTERN OF THE SIGNS OF THE ZODIAC

Sign	Gender	Element	Quality
Aries	Masculine	Fire	Cardinal
Taurus	Feminine	Earth	Fixed
Gemini	Masculine	Air	Mutable
Cancer	Feminine	Water	Cardinal
Leo	Masculine	Fire	Fixed
Virgo	Feminine	Earth	Mutable
Libra	Masculine	Air	Cardinal
Scorpio	Feminine	Water	Fixed
Sagittarius	Masculine	Fire	Mutable
Capricorn	Feminine	Earth	Cardinal
Aquarius	Masculine	Air	Fixed
Pisces	Feminine	Water	Mutable

MASCULINE AND FEMININE

These signs are said to be extrovert and introvert or yang and yin, but the theory doesn't always fit.

THE ELEMENTS: THE ESTABLISHED VIEW

Fire—Enthusiastic, impetuous, optimistic, generous
Earth—Slow, thorough, careful, dependable
Air—Ideas people, intellectuals, mentally active
Water—Intuitive, sensitive, moody

Beginners in astrology confuse the sign of Aquarius, often calling it a water sign, but it's actually an air sign. The symbol for Aquarius is the water *carrier*, hence the confusion.

THE ELEMENTS: THE INSIDE STORY

When you show fire sign people how to do something, they get it immediately. This infuriates slower colleagues.

Any woman who gets involved with an earth sign man who is married will soon discover his attitude toward major change. He won't leave his wife and family for her, and he will be even more reluctant to part with half of his estate if there's a divorce.

Air signs may or may not be intellectual, but they have strong opinions.

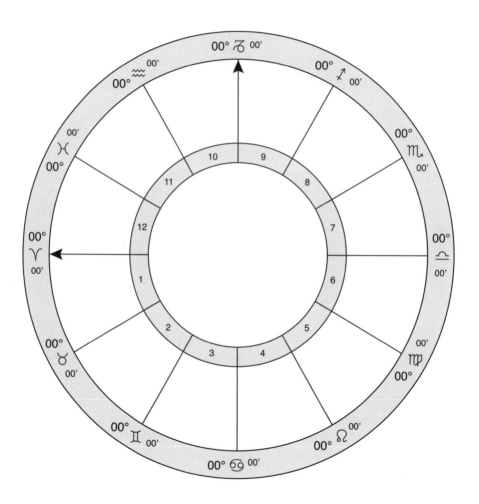

They are quick to sum up others and to spot people who might be useful to them, but they are also quick to forget their former friends.

Those who get involved with the kind, emotional, empathetic, intuitive, fascinating, and sexy water signs will have a wonderful time until they try to live or work with their lovers. The hitherto gentle and kind water signs may suddenly develop a very nasty streak, along with destructive and confrontational behavior. Water sign people insist on the freedom to float in and out of the house at will, and they often maintain a link with at least one previous lover.

THE QUALITIES: ASTRO-OPINION

The qualities are cardinal, fixed, and mutable. Cardinal people are said to initiate things, fixed people to see them through, and mutable ones to make ready for things to change.

THE QUALITIES: THE INSIDE STORY

When you look at a basic Sun sign astrology chart, and if you learn to read the symbols for the signs, you will see that the cardinal signs are those that sit at the top, bottom and to either side of the astrology chart, rather like the four points of a compass, or like the quarter hours of a clock. Thus Aries is on the left, Cancer at the bottom of the chart, Libra to the right and Capricorn is on the top.

If you consider each quadrant of the chart as a separate section, the cardinal signs are the first signs in each group, the fixed signs are the middle ones, and the mutable ones are the last ones of each group, hence the idea of initiation, stasis, and change.

Where real people are concerned, the cardinal folk like to make their own decisions, the fixed ones dislike too much change, and the mutable folk like jobs that offer a chance to meet different people from day to day and do a variety of tasks.

CHAPTER FOUR:

SIDEWAYS ASTROLOGY

Each sign of the zodiac seems to share some characteristics with the signs that border it.

ARIES
Aries shares a love of music and art with its Pisces and Taurus neighbors, while it can be as drunk as Pisces and as home-loving as Taurus.

TAURUS
Taurus can be as loud and sociable as its Aries neighbor, and also as hardworking. Taurus can also have as many varied talents, and be as interested in as many topics as any Gemini.

GEMINI

Gemini can be as family-minded as both its neighboring signs of Taurus and Cancer, and it can be as uncompromising and stubborn as they can be as well, while it worries like Cancer and socializes like Taurus.

CANCER

Cancer can be as business-minded as a Gemini and as fond of the good life as Leo. Cancerians love their children as much as a Leo, while needing change and novelty like a Gemini.

LEO

Leo can be as much into family life and as close to its parents as any Cancer, and just as interested in business. Leo can also have as high standards as any Virgo, with all the attendant Virgo fussiness. Some Leos are good teachers and some are wonderful entertainers, but they are somewhat shy and they don't like to make fools of themselves in public, so they only take to the classroom or the stage if they are certain that they know what they're doing.

VIRGO

Virgo loves to be center stage, to the point where many become actors. Virgo works as hard as any Leo, but Virgo also wants high standards of home life, luxury, and social life, like Libra does.

LIBRA

Libra is as fussy about food as a Virgo and as interested in art and literature, too. It can be as passionate about the things that interest it as any Scorpio, and as fond of arguing in public.

SCORPIO

Scorpio likes to shock people as Sagittarius does, and is as fond of traveling and seeing new things. Scorpio can be as kind as Libra and as passionate about good food, a nice home, and sex.

SAGITTARIUS

Sagittarius can be as interested in sex as Scorpio and as fond of mysticism, history, and archaeology, but it can also be as careful as Capricorn, and as reluctant to get involved with others.

CAPRICORN

Capricorn can be as fond of travel and new experiences as Sagittarius. It can also be as interested in new technology as Aquarius. Capricorn can be as independent as both its neighbors, and as interested in the psychic sciences as they are.

AQUARIUS

Aquarius can be as serious and dour as Capricorn, but also as jolly and happy—when drunk—as Pisces. Aquarius can also be as artistic, creative, and musical as Pisces.

PISCES

Pisces can be as intellectual as Aquarius and as fond of travel, new experiences, and technology, while being as determined as Aries, and as strong and independent as both its neighboring signs.

CHAPTER FIVE:
REFLECTED ASTROLOGY

An astrology chart is always drawn as a circle, so when an astrologer says that such-and-such is your opposite sign, it means that it's on the other side of the circle to yours. So if you look at the chart below, you will see that Aries is opposite to Libra, and so on around the chart.

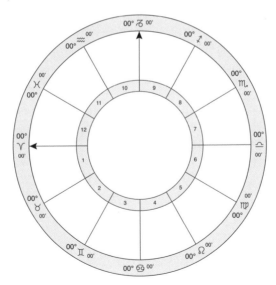

ARIES/LIBRA

Both of these signs are masculine and cardinal, which makes them strong, determined, and able to do things quickly when they want to. Both are confrontational, basically honest, and often drawn to work in a legal field.

TAURUS/SCORPIO

These are feminine, fixed signs, so both are stubborn and fond of their own opinions. Both are very capable and knowledgeable, and they can do well in business, but often prefer to hide behind a more outgoing partner.

GEMINI/SAGITTARIUS

These signs are masculine and mutable signs that are heavily into education, knowledge, and information. They both read and think deeply, and they often become friends and share interests in New Age subjects and similar issues.

CANCER/CAPRICORN

Both of these signs are cautious, family-minded, fond of their parents, and slow to change. They are into business and anything that brings money and security, but do things quickly and are very determined.

LEO/AQUARIUS

These two signs are masculine and fixed, so they are opinionated and stubborn. They both have high standards and prefer an interesting lifestyle, and they are into education for themselves and their children.

VIRGO/PISCES

These signs are feminine and mutable, so they don't look strong, yet everybody else leans upon them and expects them to come to their rescue. Neither sign likes to refuse a request, so they get used and abused, sometimes by their own family members.

CHAPTER SIX:
ASTRO-COMPATIBILITY

(OR WHAT THE SIGNS REALLY THINK ABOUT ONE ANOTHER)

Aries/Aries	• Each thinks the other is just grand.
Aries/Taurus	• Aries finds Taurus to be slow and materialistic. • Taurus considers Aries mouthy and ignorant.
Aries/Gemini	• Aries thinks Gemini is sexy and interesting. • Gemini likes Aries's sexiness.

Aries/Cancer	• Aries finds Cancer crafty but fascinating. • Cancer thinks Aries is sexy and amusing.
Aries/Leo	• Aries thinks Leo is great fun. • Leo likes Aries, until Aries inevitably turns nasty toward him.
Aries/Virgo	• Aries considers Virgo a boring fuddy-duddy. • Virgo knows that Aries is bigheaded and undisciplined.
Aries/Libra	• Aries admires Libra's sexiness and sophistication. • Libra thinks Aries leaps before looking.
Aries/Scorpio	• Aries is fascinated by Scorpio, but soon tries to compete with Scorpio. • Scorpio likes Aries's sexiness, but gets bored by Aries's childishness.

Aries/Sagittarius	• Aries respects Sagittarius's courage and adventurousness. • Sagittarius respects Aries's courage and recklessness.
Aries/Capricorn	• Aries consults Capricorn for accountancy advice. • Capricorn hires Aries to protect his property.
Aries/Aquarius	• Aries views Aquarius with contempt. • Aquarius views Aries with amusement.
Aries/Pisces	• Aries can't see how Pisces makes a living. • Pisces admires Aries's competitive streak.
Taurus/Taurus	• Each finds the other's obstinacy irritating.

Taurus/Gemini	• Taurus admires Gemini's quick mind. • Gemini admires Taurus's practicality.
Taurus/Cancer	• Taurus appreciates Cancer's concerns for his or her family. • Cancer understands Taurus's possessiveness.
Taurus/Leo	• Taurus is jealous of Leo's ability to get to the top. • Leo finds Taurus's habit of dressing in stupid clothes embarrassing.
Taurus/Virgo	• Taurus admires Virgo's ability to remember everything. • Virgo hires Taurus to fix his faulty plumbing.
Taurus/Libra	• Taurus admires Libra's homemaking skills. • Libra likes Taurus's thoroughness.

Taurus/Scorpio	• Taurus digs his or her heels in when Scorpio demands instant action. • Scorpio appreciates Taurus's practicality.
Taurus/Sagittarius	• Taurus considers Sagittarius nuts. • Sagittarius finds Taurus boring.
Taurus/Capricorn	• Taurus admires Capricorn's single-mindedness • Capricorn thinks Taurus is lazy.
Taurus/Aquarius	• Taurus thinks Aquarius talks a lot of trash. • Aquarius considers Taurus unintelligent.
Taurus/Pisces	• Taurus admires Pisces's artistic talent. • Pisces appreciates Taurus's moneymaking talent.

Gemini/Gemini	• They think the world of each other.
Gemini/Cancer	• Gemini hires Cancer to look after his or her children. • Cancer understands Gemini's concerns.
Gemini/Leo	• Gemini admires Leo's energy and enterprise. • Leo basks in Gemini's admiration.
Gemini/Virgo	• Gemini finds Virgo to be talkative. • Virgo can talk to Gemini for hours.
Gemini/Libra	• Gemini considers Libra sexy and attractive. • Libra finds Gemini sexy and attractive.

Gemini/Scorpio	• Gemini is nervous of Scorpio's sharp tongue. • Scorpio runs rings around Gemini.
Gemini/Sagittarius	• Gemini admires Sagittarius's depth of knowledge. • Sagittarius enjoys Gemini's quick mind.
Gemini/Capricorn	• Gemini works for Capricorn. • Capricorn hires Gemini to audit his books.
Gemini/Aquarius	• Gemini thinks up ideas for Aquarius to carry out. • Aquarius likes Gemini's ideas, but does nothing with them.
Gemini/Pisces	• Gemini has no time at all for Pisces. • Pisces is amazingly nasty to Gemini.

Cancer/Cancer	• These two understand each other completely.
Cancer/Leo	• Cancer admires and sometimes takes advantage of Leo. • Leo enjoys Cancer's company.
Cancer/Virgo	• Cancer hires Virgo to look after his or her children. • Virgo works for Cancer, as long as the price is right.
Cancer/Libra	• Cancer admires Libra's homemaking skills. • Libra wants more money from Cancer than he or she can give.
Cancer/Scorpio	• Cancer laughs at Scorpio's arrogance. • Scorpio thinks Cancer is soft, but this is a fight to the death.

Cancer/Sagittarius	• Cancer can't even start to understand Sagittarius. • Sagittarius likes being mothered by Cancer.
Cancer/Capricorn	• Cancer likes Capricorn's business talents. • Capricorn helps Cancer in business.
Cancer/Aquarius	• Cancer thinks Aquarius is too foolish for words. • Aquarius considers Cancer small-minded.
Cancer/Pisces	• Cancer thinks Pisces is wasting his or her life. • Pisces deems Cancer to be unadventurous.
Leo/Leo	• These two usually get on well together.

Leo/Virgo	<ul><li>Leo likes working with Virgo, as long as Leo is the boss.</li><li>Virgo likes working with Leo, as long as Leo is the boss.</li></ul>
Leo/Libra	<ul><li>Leo appreciates Libra's looks, charm, and sexuality.</li><li>Libra relies on Leo to provide money for them both.</li></ul>
Leo/Scorpio	<ul><li>Leo finds Scorpio's moodiness irritating.</li><li>Scorpio finds Leo's self-absorption irritating.</li></ul>
Leo/Sagittarius	<ul><li>Leo likes Sagittarius, but soon tires of his or her silliness.</li><li>Sagittarius finds Leo sexy and fascinating.</li></ul>
Leo/Capricorn	<ul><li>Leo enjoys having serious conversations with Capricorn.</li><li>Capricorn admires Leo's enterprise.</li></ul>

Leo/Aquarius	• Leo is rebuffed by Aquarius's coolness. • Aquarius thinks Leo is too affectionate and too needy.
Leo/Pisces	• Leo admires Pisces's creativity and salesmanship. • Pisces likes Leo's humor and sense of fun.
Virgo/Virgo	• This pair can live and work in harmony.
Virgo/Libra	• Virgo admires Libra's looks and artistry. • Libra enjoys Virgo's admiration.
Virgo/Scorpio	• Virgo wonders what capricious Scorpio will do next. • Scorpio loves Virgo's sense of humor.

Virgo/Sagittarius	• Virgo can chat with Sagittarius late into the night. • Sagittarius leaves Virgo as soon as boredom sets in.
Virgo/Capricorn	• Virgo admires Capricorn's ambition. • Capricorn hires Virgo to work out answers to tricky problems.
Virgo/Aquarius	• Virgo considers Aquarius's preoccupations stupid. • Aquarius makes Virgo angry.
Virgo/Pisces	• Virgo thinks Pisces is out of control. • Pisces thinks Virgo is too controlling toward others.
Libra/Libra	• These two have a meeting of hearts and minds.

Libra/Scorpio	• Libra is attracted by Scorpio's passion, but soon tires of Scorpio's moodiness. • Scorpio considers Libra lazy.
Libra/Sagittarius	• Libra finds Sagittarius tasteless. • Sagittarius soon dumps Libra.
Libra/Capricorn	• Libra winds Capricorn around his or her finger. • Capricorn thinks he or she can walk over Libra, but soon finds this is not the case.
Libra/Aquarius	• Libra appreciates Aquarius's sense of fun. • Aquarius loves chatting about abstract matters with Libra.
Libra/Pisces	• Libra employs Pisces to sell his products. • Pisces works for Libra, until he or she gets fed up and leaves.

Scorpio/Scorpio	• Each thinks the other is just fine.
Scorpio/Sagittarius	• Scorpio wants to possess Sagittarius, but can't. • Sagittarius enjoys fighting with Scorpio.
Scorpio/Capricorn	• Scorpio has contempt for Capricorn, but also grudging admiration. • Capricorn acts as the power behind the Scorpio throne.
Scorpio/Aquarius	• Scorpio has a grudging respect for Aquarius's cleverness. • Aquarius enjoys Scorpio's sexuality.
Scorpio/Pisces	• Sooner or later, Scorpio hurts Pisces. • Pisces wriggles out from under Scorpio's grasp.
Sagittarius/Sagittarius	• Each thinks the other is brave and fascinating.

Sagittarius/Capricorn	• Sagittarius is frustrated by Capricorn's slowness. • Capricorn considers Sagittarius irresponsible.
Sagittarius/Aquarius	• Sagittarius loves to discuss life with Aquarius. • Aquarius admires, but doesn't follow, Sagittarius's beliefs.
Sagittarius/Pisces	• Sagittarius likes to travel the world with Pisces. • Pisces enjoys Sagittarius's sense of humor.
Capricorn/Capricorn	• These two will build a business empire together.
Capricorn/Aquarius	• Capricorn thinks Aquarius is impractical. • Aquarius considers Capricorn dull.

Capricorn/Pisces	• Capricorn has contempt for Pisces. • Pisces can't wait to leave Capricorn.
Aquarius/Aquarius	• These two live and work together in harmony.
Aquarius/Pisces	• Aquarius finds Pisces extremely irritating. • Pisces ignores Aquarius's contempt and just pleases him- or herself.
Pisces/Pisces	• These two love to eat, drink, and even make love with each other.

CHAPTER SEVEN:
VIRTUES AND VICES

ARIES

- Arians choose partners when they are young and stay with them thereafter. They benefit their communities by serving on the local council or as an unpaid part-time lifeboat or fire officer, or something similar.

- Arians are restless, impatient, and can have an inflated opinion of their intelligence. They treat those whom they consider less clever or worthy than they are with contempt.

TAURUS

- Taureans are true family people who love their parents and partners deeply. They are pleasantly sociable and can be quite good listeners who don't judge others.

- Taureans can be greedy, and they don't hesitate to scrounge off others; they can be heartless enough to take from those who don't have anything to spare.

GEMINI

- Geminis are hospitable and generous to their friends. They are intelligent and good company.

- Geminis are vain and likely to spend a fortune on clothes. They have an eye on the big prize, and will even marry for money. They drop their friends as soon as someone better comes along.

CANCER

- Cancerians are good listeners and can be very sympathetic, with a knack for making those who are upset feel that they have every right to feel unhappy or put out.

- Some Cancerians are lazy, malicious, and cruel.

LEO

- Leos are hard workers who are very independent, and they don't like to ask others for any help. They will go to any lengths for their children.

- Leos can be vain and snobbish, and they have no patience with those who are weak, troubled, or unhappy.

VIRGO

- Virgos can get by on very little money, and they will take a second, third, or fourth job when necessary to keep a roof over their heads.

- Virgos set very high standards for others, but they aren't quite so particular when it comes to their own behavior.

LIBRA

- Librans are sociable and great fun to be around, stylish and nice-looking, tasteful, talented, and artistic.

- Librans can be lazy and argumentative, and they can be peculiar in unexpected ways. The only people who can live with them are strong characters who are totally weird in their own way.

SCORPIO

- Scorpios are surprisingly creative. They are fond of animals and will even do volunteer work on behalf of sick and needy animals. They can be good parents but they are truly wonderful grandparents.

- Scorpios can't stand loud noises or discomfort and will insist that others turn their music down or give up whatever they are doing if it puts the Scorpio out. They act out of emotion rather than logic, and they don't always tell the truth.

SAGITTARIUS

- Sagittarians are clever and usually cheerful. They can fix a problem in an instant, and they are kindhearted and well meaning.

- Sagittarians get bored easily and never stay anywhere for long. Don't expect them to sit around indoors or do the same thing every day.

CAPRICORN

- Capricorns don't like making an exhibition of themselves, so they never act stupidly in a social setting.

- Capricorns are snobbish and uninterested in anything or anyone that is of no real benefit to them.

AQUARIUS

- Aquarians hate injustice, so they take jobs that benefit their communities or work in advisory capacities to help others.

- Aquarians are very intense about whatever changes they have in their head at any time, but they can be utterly blind to the needs of their own children. They can be possessive and very weird.

PISCES

- Pisceans conjure up money out of nowhere when necessary, and they make a living by doing the strangest things, ranging from palmistry to tightrope-walking and to the highest level of high finance. They are wonderful parents and grandparents.

- Pisceans appear to be kind, friendly, nonjudgmental, and easygoing, but they can be stingy, spiteful, waspish, and unreliable.

CHAPTER EIGHT

SUN SIGN ARIES

MARCH 21 TO APRIL 19

Planet:	Mars
Symbol:	The Ram
Gender:	Masculine
Element:	Fire
Quality:	Cardinal
Number:	One

Before a war, military science seems a real science, like astronomy; but after a war, it seems more like astrology.
　　—Rebecca West, novelist

ARIES THINGS

Traditional astrology color	Red
Actual preferred color	Blue and beige combinations
Metal	Iron
Gem	Any red stone, such as ruby, garnet, or jasper
Likes	Cars, sports equipment
House	Lots of room for gadgets, hobbies, and mess
Vacation	A cruise, because there's no luggage restriction
Girlfriend	Anyone who brings along a plastic outfit, whip, stiletto-heeled thigh boots, and freshly pumped-up silicone boobs
Boyfriend	Someone who is deeply into spirituality, money-making, and tantric sex

THE MYTH

Arians are usually described as pioneering, intelligent, impulsive, and quick to take action. They are said to be selfish, self-centered, and always the head of the family, along with being courageous and honest. But are any of these descriptions true?

THE REALITY

Most of the above descriptions are fair, because on the whole, Arians *are* quick, intelligent, somewhat impulsive, courageous, and usually decent and honest. But *pioneering*? I can't say I've ever met a pioneering Aries. One exception that could be called a pioneer of sorts was my Aries father. He was an extremely inventive engineer who initiated some everyday objects that we see around us, such as hooded lamps that throw their light where you want it and not all around the room, the floodlight, and some forms of shop lighting. However, explorers don't seem to be thick on the ground among this sign, and a quick Internet search of obvious names turned up two Aquarians, two Pisceans, two Leos, one Cancerian, and one Virgo, but no Arians.

There isn't any evidence of great swathes of Aries people boldly going anywhere! Anyway, it would take a lot of money to make an Arian give up being able to walk to a shop and buy a newspaper or peruse high-end clothing shops at the drop of a credit card. Would they enjoy a nice walk through leach-infested jungles or schlep to the South Pole dragging a sledge? No, thanks! Well, not without several servants carrying a dozen Prada suitcases filled with their designer clothes, in addition to being assured of the chance of a decent meal and a bit of sex along the way.

Aries people like to be in dominant positions, and they can become aggressive; if they aren't allowed to be the boss, they become difficult. They have strong opinions, which they moderate while climbing up the greasy pole of politics or advancement at work. They can be know-it-alls who go on and on about politics, economics, or other subjects that they know nothing about, but their bluster often hides a lack of confidence. They don't like to be caught out in a lie.

LOOKS

Arians have charm, which makes up for their rather ordinary looks. Some women can be attractive in a small, pixie-like way when young, but they tend to become heavier when older. Arians are evenly split between being tall and angular or short and round. The men often go bald. The most obvious feature is the Aries voice. Aries men would give much to have a deep, warm voice, but most of them have a light and quiet voice at best, while some have peculiarly nasal voices.

CAREERS

Arians are very sociable, so they like to work with others and to meet lots of people during the course of their work. While they desire the top spot, they actually excel in middle management, and they like to feel that what they do is of service to humanity. Aries love politics, either on the level of water-cooler gossip or larger scale rumors and information sharing. Arians love to be in the know. Male Arians can be windbags, so along with their courage and their ability to get things done, this often leads them into the political arena.

Some years ago, an astrologer actually analyzed the Sun signs for Members of Parliament in the House of Commons in England and discovered that an amazing 45 percent of them were Arian. My guess is that many of the rest would have belonged to the adjacent sign of Pisces, or of the opposite sign of Libra.

None of the recent US presidents have been Aries, but there are millions of people working in various levels of jobs in the USA, and I would be willing to bet that a large proportion of the movers and shakers are Arians. One that did climb high—although it was via the military more than straight politics—is Colin Powell.

ARIES AT HOME

Some Arians are good housekeepers and some are excellent decorators, but there are also many of them that *think* they're good at DIY, while actually being hopeless. Part of the problem is that Aries is a starter but not a runner, so unless he or she has a partner who will actually finish the jobs that Aries starts, things somehow get left halfway through. Here are two true stories that highlight Arians' propensity to leave things unfinished.

A friend and her brand-new Aries husband, Bill, bought a pretty two-story house that had white walls and blue paintwork on the outside. As it needed some refreshing, Bill decided to do it himself. Common sense would suggest that the best way is to start at the top of the house and work down, but Bill painted the easy lower part first, choosing a disagreeable shade of mustard for the window frames and an awful brown for the walls. He couldn't be bothered to find a long ladder and do the top half of the house, so when boredom set in, he just left an uneven line between the two halves. This put the first nail into the coffin of Bill's new marriage.

Here's a remarkably similar tale that reinforces the short duration of Aries's enthusiasm. Bert decided to paint the walls going up the stairs of his new apartment. He started at the bottom, and by the time he was halfway up the steeply rising hallway, he gave up, making the place look like a real mess. Fortunately, Bert was already divorced, so there was no wife on hand for him to upset.

MORE ABOUT THE ARIES HOUSEHOLD

Some Arians are clean and tidy, but a substantial number are so filthy that even rats throw themselves on the rattraps. Here is yet another true story.

A client of mine once dated an Aries man who wore a toupee. When she visited his home, he did the usual Aries hospitality trick of tossing a ton of old newspapers off a chair, ensuring that my friend was comfortable, getting her a coffee and some cake—and then *disappearing* into some other part of the house. Getting a little bored, she reached out and picked up a newspaper that was lying on the nearest heap, only to discover one of the toupee lurking beneath, and looking for all the world like a dead ferret. She jumped out of the chair, upending the coffee mug onto the grungy carpet, and raced out, never to return.

Despite the mess in their homes, Arians' working lives are well organized, their workplaces tidy, and they are very good with paperwork.

MONEY MATTERS

Arians often display a peculiar mixture of stinginess and extravagance. They want to be seen as bighearted, but their instincts are to be careful with money. However, they can be spontaneously generous, as this next story shows.

When my children were small, I was friendly with a neighbor named Joan, who had an old car. My kids and I got around by public transportation, although Joan gave us rides in her car when possible. One day, her Aries husband astounded me. He announced that he would pay for me to be insured as a driver on Joan's car insurance and that I could borrow the car whenever I needed to. I accepted the gracious offer, always ensuring that Joan had first dibs on the car and putting much more than my share of fuel into it as a contribution toward the cost of running the car. The arrangement worked perfectly until I could afford a little used car of my own, and to this day I am grateful to this Aries man for his spontaneous generosity.

ARIES AND SEX

On the surface, Barry was a nice partner, being generous, humorous, loving, kind, and intelligent. He wasn't much in the looks department, but Rowena was happy to have someone who cared for her at long last. Barry loved sex, which was fine by Rowena, but one day he came up with a slightly bizarre proposition. Barry asked Rowena if he could hypnotize her, and she laughingly agreed. The next time they made love, Barry seemed to rush somewhat, and then went through the hypnotism spiel to put Rowena under. Rowena didn't allow herself to be taken under, but pretended she had, just to see what was next. Barry dived straight into what was obviously a long-desired fantasy, and started to act as though he were a very naughty boy, insisting that Rowena act the part of a tough nanny. Relieved that his fantasy was no worse than this, Rowena went along with it, giving Barry a well-deserved spanking. The next time she and Barry got together, he rushed through their lovemaking as fast as he could, and then got down to the *real* business of the day—more fun in the nursery. At this point, Rowena decided to end the relationship.

BODY AND HEALTH

Aries rules the head, and it does appear that Arians suffer from headaches. They can also suffer from serious eye problems, squints, and accidents that affect the eyes. Otherwise, this is a pretty healthy sign.

ARIES TRIVIA

- Arians are excellent teachers who show great patience, and they are especially good with children, although they can bully their own offspring or push them to succeed.

- Arians love expensive clothes, and they will rush out to buy something to wear the moment that they have money in their pockets. They like their families to look good, too. Having said this, not every Arian looks after his clothes once he or she has purchased them. Indeed, one wife nearly throttled her Aries husband when, still dressed in his expensive new suit, he decided to check the oil in his car with the inevitable result of smearing an oil slick down the front of his pants.

- Aries takes an amazing amount of stuff on vacation. I knew one Arian who booked a vacation in a hotel, but still took a tent along in case the room didn't suit him. I never found out whether he intended to leave the hotel and go camping or set the tent up in the bedroom and live inside it!

ARIES CELEBRITIES

- ★ Alec Baldwin
- ★ Warren Beatty
- ★ Mariah Carey
- ★ Charlie Chaplin
- ★ Tom Clancy
- ★ Russell Crowe
- ★ Doris Day
- ★ Céline Dion
- ★ Lady Gaga
- ★ Alec Guinness
- ★ Elton John
- ★ David Letterman
- ★ Ali MacGraw
- ★ Steve McQueen
- ★ Sarah Jessica Parker
- ★ Diana Ross
- ★ Steven Seagal
- ★ Ayrton Senna
- ★ Vincent van Gogh
- ★ Andrew Lloyd Webber

CHAPTER NINE:

SUN SIGN TAURUS

APRIL 20 TO MAY 20

Planet:	Venus
Symbol:	The Bull
Gender:	Feminine
Element:	Earth
Quality:	Fixed
Number:	Two

The stars which shone over Babylon and the stable in Bethlehem still shine as brightly over the Empire State Building and your front yard today.
    —Linda Goodman, astrologer / author

TAURUS THINGS

Traditional astrology color	Green, pink
Actual preferred color	Beige, black, red
Metal	Copper
Gem	Green stones, such as emerald and agate
Likes	A comfortable armchair
House	Small, neat, inexpensive house with a large garden
Vacation	Cruises and top hotels in smart cities
Girlfriend	A girl with tickets to hot events
Boyfriend	Someone the Taurean has known since childhood, so that there can be no surprises

THE MYTH

Taurus is a fixed earth sign, and therefore the most steady and reliable type of person. This is a family person who works hard in a very thorough and capable manner, as long as he or she isn't rushed. Taureans are good with their hands and thus are great cooks, wonderful gardeners, and amazing artists with a talent for home decorating. Many are happy to run a farm or work in construction. Another field that attracts Taurus is banking—home loans or anything to do with money. Astrology lore tells us that the average Taurus lacks ambition and is, frankly, rather boring. The only thing that astrological wisdom says they can do that lightens their stuffy personalities is sing.

THE REALITY

This sign can be split into two distinct groups, and by far the larger group resembles the description in the myth, albeit with a few reality checks thrown in. Taureans are extremely sociable. To my non-Taurean mind, taking a cruise would mean spending meal times with people who are not of one's own choice, which would be a form of torture to me. Taureans don't see it that way at all, and they can even cope with people they don't really like.

Most Taurus people work in a practical kind of job, like construction, recruitment, or finance. There are very few Taurean astrologers, and, interestingly, those whom I have met are either into financial astrology or herbalism and astrology. Anything to do with plants (especially ones that can be used or eaten) also fascinates them. If they are spiritual at all, this is usually within a traditional and established religion, and they can become knowledgeable about those things. Being sociable, they are quite likely to become Freemasons, Rotarians, Scout Masters or Mistresses, or something similar.

The average Taurean is better at marriage than any other sign of the zodiac, because he or she wants to be part of a happy family. Most Taureans are reasonably emotionally supportive, uncritical, and genuinely appreciative of anything that their partner does for them. Taureans aren't quite as interested in the hands-on side of parenting as other signs, but they often have the sense to find a partner who is a natural at it. Taureans have "safe hands"—their habit of moving around at a steady pace also helps them avoid dropping or walking into things. I have discovered that many Taureans work as hairdressers and makeup artists. Others make use of their combination of practicality and intellect by working in banking, home loans, investment banks, and so on. Many are careful with their own money; some are so careful that it's obvious they must have spent several previous lives in the depths of poverty.

One very strange Taurean talent that I have come across is their ability to sit absolutely still for hours, staring into space and doing nothing, not even flicking through the pages of a magazine or gazing at the television. Come to think of it, the perfect job for the so-called artistic Taurus might be an artists' model. I compare this behavior to that of an android when its power source has been switched off.

The rogue side of this sign is a fondness for embarrassing others, setting out quite deliberately to use others and even hurt them for the fun of it, just because they can.

LOOKS

The typical Taurean is of medium height and with a tendency to heaviness later in life, but if they remain active, they can stay slim. Their eyes are their best feature, and many of the men go to a lot of trouble to hide their faces under massive beards.

Venus links both Taurus and Libra to the throat and the voice, and this is supposed to make Taurus particularly interested in singing. Some sing very well, although there are far more Librans who sing and play instruments. However, I have known several Taurean folk who put their melodious voices to good use by working as hypnotherapists. Less commonly mentioned in astrology is the fact that many Taureans are also often good dancers.

THE TAUREAN DRESS AND SOCIAL CODE

Some Taurean men wear the most peculiar outfits. One wears strange, home-knitted hats and coats that are put together with odds and ends of wool, and he pairs them with saggy, baggy pants of an indeterminate grungy, grayish green. Nice!

Morris loved to shock people, so he regularly arrived at events wearing tuxedos with silver sequins on the lapels. On one occasion, he outdid even himself by showing up in full Scottish garb,. Many years ago, I heard that Morris had invited a group of suburban, respectable, rather self-satisfied married young couples to dinner. After the meal, he unrolled a screen and turned on a film projector, proceeding to entertain the assembled group with a porn film of truly graphic proportions!

CAREERS

Many Taureans choose to work in construction, furniture manufacturing, and farming or food production. Sir James Dyson, who invented the bag-free vacuum cleaner, is an example. He's said to be stubborn and a hard businessman who is now a billionaire.

Many are reliable and capable low- or mid-range workers with little ambition, but I've met quite a lot who are really best at lying around, chatting with friends, and watching TV. Most Taureans are very reliable, turning up for work every day, even if they are not feeling well, and invariably being cheerful, competent, and a credit to their employers. Taureans love animals, and one Taurus friend even takes her dog to work with her!

TAURUS AT HOME

In the majority of cases, the Taurus home is tidy, pleasant, and indeed the epitome of suburban living. Taurus people and their homes could easily be used for those retro television commercials that show a housewife, complete with a frilly apron, but there are exceptions. Lynne and Peter were both Taurean, and they had an expensive but casually decorated home, complete with uncomfortable, unmatched secondhand couches and a 1950s wicker chair that dangled from a chain in the middle of the room. Their main interest was in their two massive and totally undisciplined dogs, especially the lively dalmatian that always made a beeline to sniff every woman visitor.

Another exception to the pleasant home situation was Russell. Russell lived alone (thankfully), and he turned his house into a combination of construction site and motorbike repair shop. He combined two small rooms into one larger one by knocking a hole in the adjoining wall, but leaving the remaining brickwork in a ragged mess.

FIXED IDEAS

A typical Taurean trait is stubbornness, and this can sometimes lead to very fixed opinions. For instance, Valerie had a fanatical hatred of Nazis, and this translated into a deep loathing for anything or anyone from Germany. Valerie wasn't Jewish and she had no Jewish friends or relatives, but she managed to bring the Holocaust into every conversation.

A LACK OF DIGNITY

One trait often shared by all three of the earth signs (Taurus, Virgo, and Capricorn) that I can't get my head around, is the belief that other people should provide for them. Virgo will suggest going out for dinner, then sit back and expect you to pay for it; Capricorn is impossible to do business with to any kind of *mutual* advantage; Taurus likes to ask for what it wants. Here are two examples:

Taurean Nicola was far from rich, but she had a massive garden that needed landscaping. Nicola did occasional work for a woman named Claire who owned a small business. Claire happened to be in financial trouble and made no secret of it, but to Nicola's mind, if someone had their own business, it stood to reason that they were rich. Nicola phoned Claire and demanded that she give her money against possible future work that Nicola might or might not do. Claire tried reasoning with Nicola, to the point of actually offering to send her copies of her bank statements, but to no avail. The Taurean obstinacy meant that Nicola wouldn't shut up, so Claire hung up and shut her out of her life.

Greta makes craft projects out of bits of material, stones, and seeds. Those who are unlucky enough to encounter Greta in a social setting are guaranteed to have her dreadful projects pushed at them for their inspection. When the poor victim makes a polite comment about the stuff being very nice, Greta pounces. She purposely assumes that they want to buy and tells them how much they owe her, knowing that the embarrassment factor will kick in and the unsuspecting victim will be sure to hand over the money. Greta's motto is, "Never leave home without the crap pile, because the next unwilling customer may be just around the corner!"

To be fair, not all Taureans are like this, and most are great company. But none that I have ever met are truly generous.

BODY AND HEALTH

The weak spots are said to be the lower jaw, the throat, and the neck, and there is a tendency toward diabetes, especially in those who put on weight. Despite the fact that there is nothing in astrology to account for it, many Taurus people suffer with arthritis in the knees.

TAURUS TRIVIA

- Taureans are often lucky, and can inherit large sums of money. Once they have enough, they spend time on their hobbies, socializing and talking.

- Taureans are surprisingly good with computers.

- Reports from friends who have been involved with Taurean men and women are that they are good lovers.

- Taurus likes its own way, and it can be as aggressive as any Aries, but in a stubborn manner.

- If ripped off, Taureans fly into a rage. (Not that they are alone in this!)

- Taureans rarely make a career out of astrology, spiritual or psychic matters, but they have an easygoing attitude toward it, rarely being against any of the psychic sciences.

TAURUS CELEBRITIES

- ★ David Beckham
- ★ Cher
- ★ Che Guevara
- ★ George Clooney
- ★ Penélope Cruz
- ★ Bob Dylan
- ★ Ella Fitzgerald
- ★ Henry Fonda
- ★ Katharine Hepburn
- ★ Adolf Hitler
- ★ Janet Jackson
- ★ Shirley MacLaine
- ★ Willie Nelson
- ★ Jack Nicholson
- ★ Al Pacino
- ★ Michelle Pfeiffer
- ★ Tori Spelling
- ★ Barbra Streisand
- ★ Uma Thurman
- ★ Harry S. Truman

SUN SIGN GEMINI

MAY 21 TO JUNE 21

Planet:	Mercury
Symbol:	The Twins
Gender:	Masculine
Element:	Air
Quality:	Mutable
Number:	Three

Astrology is one of the earliest attempts made by man to find the order hidden behind or within the confusing and apparent chaos that exists in the world.
   —Karen Hamaker-Zondag, leading astrologer / author

GEMINI THINGS

Traditional astrology color	Yellow
Actual preferred color	Black, pale blue
Metal	Mercury
Gem	Lace agate, citrine
Likes	Bags, cases, briefcases, purses
House	A neat retreat with an office attached
Vacation	A good hotel in a sunny area
Girlfriend	Someone else's wife
Boyfriend	Someone who is willing to get married

THE MYTH

This is said to be a many-sided, scatterbrained sign that gets involved with a number of jobs, hobbies, tasks, and interests, but doesn't finish any of them. Gemini is supposedly restless, fascinated by new situations and new people, and unable to sit still or stay in one place for long. The name of the game for this sign is communication, so Geminis are said to write letters, keep in touch with everyone, talk nonstop, and travel all the time. Being generous, friendly, and flirty, Geminis have thousands of friends.

THE REALITY

Whenever I meet a new Gemini in some social setting, they make a point of telling me that their sign is schizophrenic and that they have two sides to their character. Well, they aren't alone in this—most of us have two or more sides to our natures, and I haven't noticed Gemini being any more double-sided than many other Sun sign types. Most Geminis are intelligent and quick-minded, but they speak rather slowly, so they don't come across as especially bright. Many of them find it hard to make up their minds or come to an important decision, so perhaps this is where the two-sided effect kicks in, because while one side of them wants change, the other side wants things to stay as they are.

Astrology tells us that Gemini and its sister sign of Virgo are both ruled by Mercury, which is the planet of communication. While many Geminis actually teach—anything from tiny children to older ones—or train adults as part of their job, they aren't especially communicative in other ways, and most are actually secretive! Not only are they good at keeping their own secrets and those of others, but they are often secretive when it isn't necessary, or even when it's counterproductive.

Geminis are heavily into family life, and they try to keep their families together at all costs. Many Geminis endure difficult childhoods, where family life doesn't really exist or where they are square pegs in round holes. When they grow up, they try hard to create a happy family, fully equipped with a partner, children, and a nicely appointed home base. Young Gemini girls dream about a future that includes a wedding, a nice little house, a loving husband, and several gorgeous babies. They have a visceral need for this, because it was probably missing in their early life. I also truly believe that many Geminis have had several past lives where they lost families or lost their way in life, so having and keeping a stable home and family are very important to them. However, even in this life, it doesn't always work out that well for them—although in some cases they are lucky this time around, and manage to find and keep what they want.

Even those who have a reasonably good home life during childhood may be bullied at school. There's always something that makes the Gemini jittery, unsettled, unsafe, and worried when young, and it often spills over into adulthood, even making them somewhat neurotic. Sometimes this ends up causing a chronic condition that is aggravated by stress, such as asthma or bronchitis. In days gone by, most Geminis smoked, and that didn't help their poor lung function, as well as damaging their already-vulnerable teeth. There seems to be a lot of karma for this sign to live through.

LOOKS

Geminis are small. While some are overweight, many aren't really into food and therefore stay thin throughout life, either being fashionably birdlike or skinny, depending on one's point of view. Their best features are their heart-shaped faces and large eyes, but Geminis of both sexes spend a lifetime being martyrs to their hair and teeth, and have to spend a fortune on both. Some have such an undercut lower jaw and small chin that they need several years of treatment in adolescence to correct this. In addition, their hands look old even when they are still young.

THEIR OWN WORST ENEMIES

Gemini is a mutable sign, and the word *mutable* implies adaptability. However, this just isn't borne out by reality, because Geminis find it hard to adapt, compromise, or see another point of view. Their worst trait is a tendency to whine and complain, and this is aggravated by the fact that many have an irritating, tinny, and whiny tone to their voices, often with the resigned sigh of the truly put-upon being just a hair's breadth away. They can be negative, pessimistic, and extremely sorry for themselves. They relive past hurts, and if they drink alcohol, that exacerbates the situation. Some Geminis nag, complain, and criticize, none of which endear them to their spouses or their children.

Despite being a mutable sign, Geminis are surprisingly fixed. For instance, once they have decided to fall in love, they hang in there for decades in the hopes that the person they love will give them the commitment they want. Jess's story is not unusual: Gemini Jess was in love with Peter. Jess was a divorcée with one child, while Peter was married with three children. He swore that he would leave his wife for Jess once his youngest child left school, but when the time came, he refused to make the move. Eventually, even loyal Jess gave up waiting and found someone else.

MYSTERIES ABOUND

There can be weird and mysterious events in the Gemini life. Witness one old friend named Linda, who broke the Gemini trend by having good parents and a happy marriage. When Linda was already middle-aged, she accidentally discovered that she wasn't her parents' firstborn child—there had been a boy born before her, but he had died in infancy.

AS PARENTS

Gemini parents mean well, but they may enlist their children in marital fights, thus making their children unhappy and ensuring that the kids leave home at an early age to escape the chaos. Some mothers are astonishingly bossy and continue to push their children around long after the children have grown up. Despite this, their adult children are often very good to them.

THE WORLD IS FULL OF MARRIED COUPLES

Married Geminis often have another attachment that they keep going on the side for many years. Gemini females make up a fair proportion of a consultant astrologer's clientele, and they keep coming back year after year, hoping that *this* will be the year when the astrologer tells them that their man-friend will leave his wife for them. From the outside, it's sad to see such silliness.

Sometimes the female Gemini is perfectly faithful to her husband, but the man has one girlfriend after another throughout the marriage. Here is another true story: Ivy had long since accepted that her Gemini husband, Leon, was a womanizer. Although she was quite a sexy woman herself, she couldn't keep up with Leon's sex drive—no single female could—so she was actually quite relieved when Leon had someone else on the side, because he would vanish for a while, leaving her to relax at home with her favorite soap operas and without him fussing around the place. She knew that Leon would never leave her, that he wasn't emotionally attached to any of his girlfriends, and that he was too cheap to spend real money on them. Therefore, she looked upon his occasional vanishing acts in the way that other women understand their husbands' need to spend time playing golf or fishing.

Gemini men do tend to vanish for days on end, because they get bored and restless if they go through the same routine day after day. Sometimes, a bad day at work sets their nerves jangling and makes them want to escape normal life for a while. Some happily married Gemini men are eternally busy outside the home with their sports, Freemasonry, projects or hobbies, or any one of a hundred other things.

Joe was a gay friend of mine, and he lived with Gemini Craig. Every now and then Craig would go out for a pack of cigarettes and vanish off the face of the earth, only to turn up again several days later, walking in the door as though nothing had happened. Joe wasn't worried because he'd gotten used to Craig's peculiarities, and Joe knew that Craig would feel more settled and in control of his life after returning from his little excursion. Joe even knew more or less where Craig had gone.

CAREERS

Many Gemini men work in a therapeutic field, such as medicine, complementary medicine, psychology, dentistry, and so on. Bizarrely, this is never mentioned in astrology books or among astrologers. Others work in obvious Gemini jobs, such as telephone operator, taxi driver, or temporary office worker. Many professional tennis players are Geminis, which makes sense, as this sign rules the shoulders, arms, and hands.

BODY AND HEALTH

Gemini rules the upper chest, bronchial tubes, shoulders, arms, and hands. It's true that Geminis do tend to get a lot of colds and coughs, and quite a lot of them suffer from asthma. This isn't helped by the fact that many of them smoke. Geminis break their hands, arms, wrists, and elbows, also tending to get arthritis in these areas. Many suffer years of dental work due to badly shaped jaws, in particular a bad overbite or a very short lower jaw.

GEMINI TRIVIA

- Gemini women are often attracted to Aries or Libra men. They try to tame them, but it never works.

- Geminis like a change of scene, but their homes are important to them. Most keep their houses very neat and tidy, because they are actually very proud of them.

- Some Geminis are funny about food (i.e. becoming vegetarian) or very fussy about what they will and won't eat. Some prefer chocolate or wine to food any day.

- Most Geminis are fond of animals, and they tend to have pets, especially cats. I often think that cats (with their independence, need for freedom, and clean, fussy ways) are themselves the epitome of Geminis.

GEMINI CELEBRITIES

- ★ Annette Bening
- ★ George H. W. Bush
- ★ Joan Collins
- ★ Tony Curtis
- ★ Johnny Depp
- ★ Judy Garland
- ★ Steffi Graf
- ★ John F. Kennedy
- ★ Nicole Kidman
- ★ Anna Kournikova

- ★ Barry Manilow
- ★ Dean Martin
- ★ Sir Paul McCartney
- ★ Marilyn Monroe
- ★ Ralph Nader
- ★ Natalie Portman
- ★ Joan Rivers
- ★ Brooke Shields
- ★ Donald Trump

CHAPTER ELEVEN:
SUN SIGN CANCER

JUNE 22 TO JULY 22

Planet:	The Moon
Symbol:	The Crab
Gender:	Feminine
Element:	Water
Quality:	Cardinal
Number:	Four

Who needs astrology? The wise man gets by on fortune cookies.
   —Edward Abbey, author

CANCER THINGS

Traditional astrology color	White, silver
Actual preferred color	Any shade of blue
Metal	Silver
Gem	Pearls, milky white stones
Likes	Chocolate
House	An ordinary house with a large yard or garden for the kids
Vacation	Anywhere near or on the sea
Girlfriend	A pretty girl who never looks at another man
Boyfriend	A tall man with lots of hair

THE MYTH

Cancer is deemed to be clingy, home-loving, fond of its mother, and similar to the mother in looks and nature. This sign supposedly loves its own children and its family as a whole. Cancer is said to be a great cook and a wonderful homemaker, but also clever at running a small business. Most of all, this sign is considered to be emotional, softhearted, protective, very intuitive, and inclined to crawl into its shell. Astrologers tell us that this is a gentle, touchy-feely, maternal sign that loves nothing better than making cakes for its family and spreading love and light around in abundance.

THE REALITY

Cancerians have a reputation for being protective of themselves and those they love, and in this case, the myth and reality do match. Cancerians are led by their emotions, so when they are happy, they can be wonderful company, but when they are angry, disappointed, or unhappy, they externalize their emotions by making others suffer. This is a very black-and-white sign that can inspire great love or great hatred in others.

Cancerians can say one thing and then do something else, or they can go about things in such convoluted ways that nobody knows what the outcome might be. This is a cardinal sign and thus unlikely to be influenced by anything other than its own desires and requirements. Cancer people are efficient and effective, but they can be lazy and not really get around to anything if they don't feel inspired. Cancerian charm, diplomacy, salesmanship, and apparent softness make them look easy to push around, but they aren't.

A friend of mine once commented that her daughter's Cancerian boyfriend was moody and possessive, and I would add that too often they can be cruel, unfeeling, and extremely hurtful. Cancerians despise weakness, and they view those in a weak position as being beneath contempt. If others become dependent upon them, they can make their lives a misery. This makes many of them impossible as a boss, stepparent, in-law, and, in some cases, neighbor. They take whatever self-protective strategies they learned from childhood into adulthood, to use as weapons against others when it's no longer appropriate or necessary. The following true story has stuck in my head for many years:

When I was working in an office, I met into a young secretary, and I couldn't help noticing that she was extremely distressed. It turned out that she had a new Cancerian boss who was bullying her unmercifully. Apparently, shortly before coming to the firm, this nasty piece of work had been an officer in the navy. (I strongly suspected that he'd been kicked out). Once home from the sea, his wife faced the appalling prospect of him being a permanent presence in her household, so she promptly left. Luckily, an old pal wrangled a managerial job for the man at our firm, but he was unsuited to the work and uninterested in it. What he really wanted was his old life back. Okay, the man was at a low point, but why take it out on a nineteen-year-old secretary who was in no position to stand up to him? Cancerians really do need to take more care, because they can build up some hideous karma for themselves.

Cancerians are cautious; they don't make decisions easily and they fear losing their security, so they can't bring themselves to gamble or take chances on anything. They can sit things out to the point where they don't really live their lives, but just go through the motions. One thing that can move them emotionally is falling in love. They have vivid imaginations and deep feelings that can be aroused when love, lust, and romance enter their lives. Some can use this to their benefit by writing romantic books or scripts for television and film, and some are surprisingly artistic. The cooks among this sign express their love of beauty by making attractive meals, decorating wonderful wedding cakes, or helping people to arrange terrific weddings.

THE OTHER SIDE OF THE COIN

I have had some marvelous Cancerian friends whose loyalty, kindness, generosity, and emotional support kept me going through some very tough times. One friend died last year, and I miss her wisdom, unfailing loyalty, friendship, and understanding every single day. More than anything, I miss her wonderful sense of humor and her ability to see the funny side of life.

I have known people of this sign who are good to their relatives, friends, and work colleagues. I have another friend with whom I often work, and I trust her completely, as she is a very good person, which goes to show the extremes that this sign runs to. Another friend was married to a Cancerian man. I considered him a lazy user who loved to upset others, but my friend loved her Cancer husband to bits and forgave his every sin, so he obviously had something going for him.

LOOKS

Cancerians are usually quite tall, so even though they put on weight later in life, they carry it well. Cancerian faces are rather long, and while both sexes are fairly attractive when young, they tend to look distinctly bovine as they age.

CANCER AT HOME

Cancerian extremes of behavior show up in their homes, as you will see from the following true stories:

Crystal had three sons and then found herself pregnant with an unwanted fourth child; this turned out to be yet another son, and she took her anger and disappointment out on the poor kid, never forgiving him for having been born.

Janet took on the responsibility for her two grandsons after her own son deserted his wife and the wife couldn't cope with the situation; she did a really good job.

Gwen looked after her sick husband for years, while she also earned the money that made their lives comfortable.

CAREERS

Cancerians are great at providing things that the public needs, so you will find them in catering, running coffee shops, bars, restaurants, and so on. I've known quite a few who own and run food trucks. At the other end of the economic scale, Cancerian Richard Branson, the Virgin Airways mogul, also provides fast food and transport services to the public.

Astrology tells us that this sign is particularly interested in history and that they enjoy coin and antique collecting, but I can't see it. The Cancer mind is attuned to finding workable answers to tricky questions rather than studying hallmarks or learning to distinguish the precise design of something.

COSMIC ORDERING

A few years ago, a woman wrote a book proposing the theory that all we have to do to get what we want out of life is to mentally ask for things, and then sit back and wait for our cosmic orders to drop into our laps. Apparently the author used the technique herself to acquire a perfect husband, a perfect home, and great wealth. Well, my guess is that the author must be a Cancer, because if anybody can pull this kind of thing off, they can. (After writing the above paragraph, I checked out the author's star sign, and guess what? It's Cancer!) Those of us who belong to the other eleven signs can long for the things we need or want all day long, but they just won't drop into our laps.

After her husband moved out and the divorce was under way, Juliet decided that the best place for her three sons was a top-level boarding school. Juliet figured that her ex could finance part of the cost, and that she could access whatever scholarships were available for the remainder. Neighbors muttered that she had no chance of making this happen, especially as the oldest boy was clearly not a good student, but when Juliet put her mind to something, she could move mountains. Sure enough, by the start of the following school year, the oldest boy was safely enrolled in the school, soon to be followed by his younger brothers.

CALMNESS UNDER FIRE

Cancerians have one very enviable trait, which is that they rarely if ever get emotionally upset about anything at work. Even when the local bully decides to pick on them, it goes in one ear and out the other, and they take criticism as a compliment. Noise and disturbance in the workplace doesn't bother them. If there is some kind of bad atmosphere at work, the Cancerian can magically calm the situation down, using powers of tact and diplomacy that are utterly amazing. All ambassadors, UN negotiators, and hostage negotiators should be Cancerian.

BODY AND HEALTH

At one point, there was such fear of the word *cancer* that astrologers started to refer to Cancerians as Moon Children. Do Cancerians get cancer? Of course they do, but so does everyone else. This sign rules the breasts, chest, lungs, and stomach. Many of them suffer from arthritis.

CANCER TRIVIA

- Cancerians have great ideas, but little follow-through, and while some are hardworking and reliable, others are lazy.

- This is an extremely patriotic sign, so these folk will fight hard for their country.

- Cancerian hearing is usually good throughout life, and it can be so sensitive that they don't like noises and they need to live in a reasonably quiet environment. They also have good memories.

- Like all water signs, Cancerians are intuitive and often psychic.

- Cancerians don't like to waste money and they can be stingy, but they can spend it like water if there's something they really want.

- Cancer folk need a base. They can't live on other people's couches; they need their own space. They aren't tied to their homes, though, as they like to travel and to visit relatives and friends who live elsewhere.

- These folk are great listeners, and this makes them wonderful healers, medics, counselors, arbitrators, or anything else that requires real listening and understanding. This is a rare skill.

CANCER CELEBRITIES

- ★ 50 Cent
- ★ Pamela Anderson
- ★ Richard Branson
- ★ Gisele Bündchen
- ★ George W. Bush
- ★ Tom Cruise
- ★ the Dalai Lama
- ★ Vin Diesel
- ★ Harrison Ford
- ★ Tom Hanks
- ★ Courtney Love
- ★ Nelson Mandela
- ★ Angela Merkel
- ★ George Michael
- ★ Camilla Parker Bowles
- ★ Sylvester Stallone
- ★ Ringo Starr
- ★ Meryl Streep
- ★ Prince William
- ★ Robin Williams

CHAPTER TWELVE:

SUN SIGN LEO

JULY 23 TO AUGUST 22

Planet:	The Sun
Symbol:	The Lion
Gender:	Masculine
Element:	Fire
Quality:	Fixed
Number:	Five

I don't believe in astrology. The only stars I can blame for my failures are those that walk about the stage.
   —Noel Coward, playwright / actor

LEO THINGS

Traditional astrology color	Gold, yellow, orange
Actual preferred color	Any bright shade
Metal	Gold
Gem	Diamond, topaz, tiger's eye
Likes	Fast, expensive cars
House	Large, open plan, modern, with room for all the children's junk
Vacation	A top-class vacation complex with a good swimming pool
Girlfriend	A classy woman who won't embarrass you when out and about
Boyfriend	Very classy, intelligent, sexy, and wealthy

THE MYTH

Leos are convinced of their importance, loyal only to themselves, and fond of taking center stage because they consider themselves higher than royalty. One astrologer has said that a Leo expects people to stand up and sing the "Hallelujah" chorus when he enters a room.

THE REALITY

Leo is a sign that really does polarize, with a small minority being unbelievably awful, the majority good-natured, and most being the absolute salt of the earth. Leaving aside the unpleasant ones for the moment and concentrating on the normal ones, Leos are somewhat shy, although they cover it up well; they don't like being the center of attention, but neither do they enjoy being ignored. Leos are good teachers who enjoy lecturing on subjects with which they are familiar, and it is this circumstance that makes them a focus of attention, because in order to teach, one needs to stand up in front of others and talk.

Leos have high standards, and that makes them excellent employees. They turn up for work day after day, even if they are ill or bored by the job, and they carry out every task to the best of their ability. They are honest, reliable, and decent. Leos are no more talented than any other sign of the zodiac, but they are organized, businesslike, and fair. As employers or business owners, they ensure that all parties in a project get their due share of the income, rather than simply looking after their own interests. The kind of small-minded, thieving nastiness that brings so many people up in front of Judge Judy is alien to the average Leo.

Most Leos have pretty good childhoods, although their parents might be somewhat old-fashioned or authoritarian, so they grow up knowing the boundaries. They try to recreate this with their own families, giving vast amounts of love to their partners and children, but refusing to stand for bad behavior. Being a fixed sign, it takes a lot to make Leos leave a partnership or a job, so even if things aren't great, they'll stay put and see it through. They offset their frustrations with a good old complaining session with their friends, but their sense of humor and sense of balance soon kicks back in again. Surprisingly for a fixed sign, Leos are adaptable and easygoing within marriage and personal relationships, so they tend to make their partners happy. They certainly put those who they love before themselves. Love means a lot to Leos, and they take their responsibilities seriously.

A LEO BUTTON

There are people who I call "turners." Those who don't have the Sun in Leo may not recognize this as a problem, but it's one that Leos can't tolerate. Turners are your very best friends for several years, until they suddenly "turn" and have no further use for you. When you ask them what you've done to them, they look at you as though you were some weird, smelly stranger. As far as Leo is concerned, the moment that trust leaves a friendship or a relationship, it's the end of the road. Here is a true example:

Leo Alexa and Gemini Tania were firm friends. Alexa helped Tania train for a new career and put her life together again after various divorces and upsets, including spending many hours comforting Tania while she cried and complained about her love life. Then Tania found what she *really* needed in life, which was a man with money in the bank, who offered her his hand in marriage rather than the usual one-night-stand scenario. The fact that he was undersized, with a red face, strangely inward-facing teeth, a Hitler mustache, and a clear problem with alcohol didn't matter to Tania.

Overnight, Alexa became surplus to Tania's requirements because she just didn't need Alexa's friendship anymore, and when Alexia tried to talk to Tania about this, Tania turned cold and nasty. She did invite Alexa to her wedding, but sat her in an obscure corner and treated her like dirt, scowling and turning her back when Alexa tried to talk to her. Alexa left the wedding early and had nothing more to do with Tania after that.

If you have Leo friends, bear in mind that they will be the most loyal and helpful pals in the world as long as you don't turn on them. Simple, isn't it?

LEOS BEHAVING BADLY

Like many signs, this one contains saints and sinners. The truly rotten ones are unbearable, and their nastiness is often a mix of crafty self-interest and dense stupidity, so much so that one wonders whether they had been dropped on their heads shortly after birth. Here are a couple real life examples:

Leo Oliver was a fast-talking businessman, in the vein of a used car salesman, but his line of work was computers. This was in the early days of computers, and Oliver could rely on the fact that most of his customers didn't know one end of a machine from another, so he sold them broken garbage for a hefty profit. He had a habit of starting a business, getting credit, going bankrupt, and then starting up something else and doing the same again.

Leo Sheila was a large woman with a very large chest, and she was always done-up, complete with glittery turquoise eye shadow and a helmet hairdo that was firmly glued in place with half a can of hairspray. When she entered a room, she looked like a large ship in full sail. If she came near a female, she didn't stop, but passed right by, tossing out pleasantries such as, "You've put on weight," or "Haven't I seen you in that dress before?" When she came across a man, she halted and simpered prettily, convinced that any man couldn't help but fall directly under her spell. Sheila's long-suffering husband might have been an object of pity if he weren't so spiteful.

Leo Frazer was a bully who had inherited a great deal of money, so in his eyes, he was a very important man. He and his girlfriend Mavis tried to impress others by buying them lavish meals and then sneering and ridiculing their guests throughout the meal.

LOOKS

The rules of astrology tell us that Leos have hair like a lion's mane, and there are some Leos who do, but many have hair that is soft and won't stay in place for long. Leo women don't worry too much about their hair, but Leo men, on the other hand, can get into a dreadful state. I've known several Leo men who have gone through phases of having their hair permanently waved and colored.

CHILDHOOD

Leos can be very sick when young, and before the days of antibiotics and decent medicine, many Leo children didn't make it to adulthood. Leo babies are slow to sit up and walk; however, Leo teens take to driving like ducks to water, so it's my belief that they decide early in life that they're not going to move around until they have wheels to do it with. If you take a Leo child out for the day, take a stroller along, because these children soon tire. Some Leo children don't lose even one tooth until well into their second year, and take their time to develop in many other ways, too. Yet they are far from mentally slow. Many compensate for their late motor development by talking when very young indeed. My Leo children both started to talk at seven months, and by eighteen months, both were capable of holding quite a complex conversation (including talking back, and arguing).

Leo's natural disinclination to study means they do badly at school, but once they get a bit older, something seems to click. Sometimes it's a particular subject that piques their interest, but often they just make the connection between good test results and a good job and the money to buy the lifestyle that they want. Many Leos leave school early, work for a while, and then go back to college later, irritating their long-suffering parents by passing every exam in sight with honors. Barack Obama is a typical example.

AS PARENTS

The following story is by no means an extreme example of the deep love that Leos have for their offspring. Dave lived in England, and was divorced with two small children, whom he looked after every other weekend. Suddenly he was offered a job in Toronto, so he negotiated with his employers that he would take every other Friday off, making up the time during the interim weekends if need be. Every other Friday, Dave would board a plane, fly to England, and spend the weekend with his children, flying back to Toronto on Sunday night—and all this at his own expense!

CAREERS

Leos are well organized and hardworking, and they have a knack for business. They aren't natural salespeople, but they can sell as long as they believe in the product. Leos have a natural affinity with computers, and they understand the principles of engineering, although they aren't usually hands-on engineers. Many become teachers, either teaching children, working in adult education, working as trainers for sports, or giving training for a specific job. Many of them love to grow flowers, fruit, and vegetables as a hobby, and as a relief from the stress of their business careers.

BODY AND HEALTH

Leos are either very fit or they suffer constantly with their health, although they rarely take time off work or give in to health problems. The sign traditionally rules the heart and the spine, and many Leos suffer from spinal problems, often as a result of an accident. This isn't reserved for the lumbar area, as problems can arise in any part of the spine from the skull to the tail. Leos can also suffer from arthritis and other inflammatory bone problems in various parts of the body. Leos do have more heart problems than other signs and fewer instances of cancer than others. Serious inflammatory problems can also affect the digestion and the bowels.

LEO TRIVIA

- These people hate making a scene or being in the middle of someone else's drama.

- If you ridicule a Leo, he or she will never forgive you.

- They are good swimmers, and women can't cope with ball games, while men will play an occasional game of tennis or pool, but no team games.

- A Leo won't put up with a partner, however nice, if they are not good in bed.

- Leos have a reputation for snobbery, and this is borne out by fact.

- Leos are very clean and they hate having sticky hands or dirty hair; if their hair is not right, they are extremely unhappy.

LEO CELEBRITIES

- ★ Ben Affleck
- ★ Antonio Banderas
- ★ Halle Berry
- ★ Sandra Bullock
- ★ Bill Clinton
- ★ Robert de Niro
- ★ Roger Federer
- ★ Melanie Griffith
- ★ Whitney Houston
- ★ Mick Jagger
- ★ Jennifer Lopez
- ★ Madonna
- ★ Barack Obama
- ★ Sean Penn
- ★ Daniel Radcliffe
- ★ Robert Redford
- ★ Arnold Schwarzenegger
- ★ Patrick Swayze
- ★ Charlize Theron
- ★ Mae West

CHAPTER THIRTEEN:
SUN SIGN VIRGO

AUGUST 23 TO SEPTEMBER 22

Planet:	Mercury & Chiron
Symbol:	The Maiden
Gender:	Feminine
Element:	Earth
Quality:	Mutable
Number:	Six

The only function of economic forecasting is to make astrology look respectable.
—John Kenneth Galbraith, world-renowned Economist

VIRGO THINGS

Traditional astrology color	Cinnamon shades
Actual preferred color	Gray, shades of plum or wine
Metal	Mercury
Gem	Purple stones, such as amethyst
Likes	A large tank of tropical fish, a good kitchen
House	Enough room to escape from the other family members
Vacation	Places with a lot of history, such as Egypt, England or China
Girlfriend	Any attractive woman with bisexual tendencies
Boyfriend	Someone with a good job

THE MYTH

Virgos are quiet, modest with regard to food and drink, frigid, and virginal. They are excessively neat and tidy, and they spend their lives devoting themselves to the needs of others. Virgos are into health matters and public health, leading them into careers in hospitals or working for charities that benefit humanity. Their downfalls are extreme neurosis and a tendency to criticize others. Astrologers tell us that Leo is the show-off while Virgo lurks at the back of the room, twisting their hands in embarrassment at being out at a social occasion.

THE REALITY

Virgos are clever, and their minds hold whole encyclopedias of information, which they can access at the speed of light, so they can be guaranteed to win quizzes. Some are devoted to the service of others, and many work in health services, or in other ways that benefit humanity. They often take up with people who need to be rescued, such as drinkers who fear losing control, so Virgos actually become the consciences and saviors of others.

Many Virgos are dedicated to their careers, and they can become quite wealthy due to their brainpower and capacity for long hours and hard work. Many adore being the center of attention and having others hanging on to their words, or admiring them for their wisdom. Virgos thoroughly enjoy social gatherings, and they can drink a bit too much and then thoroughly amuse everyone who's around them.

While some are family people, my experience is that Virgos do better in a kind of loose arrangement, where they have some kind of partner, but don't need to spend much time with them. They can be deeply into their jobs or volunteer work, or just doing too many things at once. These Virgos treat their homes like a pit stop where they rest and refuel their shattered nerves before getting ready to go out again. Others work from home, with lots of people passing through the place so that there's always someone interesting to talk to. Virgos make wonderful friends, and they don't like to let their friends down. They also have the most wonderful sense of humor.

TIDINESS

The famed Virgo tidiness is a myth, but Virgos have a photographic memory, so they know exactly how to find everything in the bombsite that passes for their office. Virgos hate it when someone cleans up their stuff or interferes with their territory. On one occasion, our Jon took pity on a friend who needed somewhere to stay, and she thought she would repay his generosity by painting his kitchen, which in her opinion needed to be completely redesigned. Unfortunately, she didn't warn Jon about this, but just waited until he went out for the day. He came home that evening to find his kitchen sky blue, and he went ballistic, swiftly throwing the unfortunate woman out.

LOOKS

Virgos can be anything from average in height to tall and rather good-looking, with good bone structure. Most of them age well. They rarely gain much weight even though they dislike exercise, other than walking around while shopping. They can have uneven teeth and spend a lot of time at the dentist throughout life. Many have flimsy, flyaway hair, while some have very curly hair that they may dislike.

CHILDHOOD

Virgos seem to choose a difficult karma before birth, sometimes endowing them with parents who often aren't the best of parents. Sometimes they are harsh and demanding, while others have are snobbish and overly concerned about what the neighbors think, often being obsessed with cleanliness and housework. Some have parents who are ruled by obsessive beliefs, which may be religious or political. The parents of a Virgo child lack common sense and a sense of balance. Virgos work tirelessly for any tiny measure of approval and the teeniest sniff of parental love. If they become the perfect A student, the most successful athlete, the most gifted artist, the most pious rabbi, or have the neatest room in creation, the parents move the goalposts so that the poor child must strive hard all over again.

PERFECTIONISM

Even without such parental pressure, Virgo children are studious, clever, modest, easily shamed, and they can be plagued by their own high standards. They can be highly critical of others, highly self-critical, and overly perfectionist, and they hate feeling that they are falling down on a job. They expect perfection from themselves and they can be very hard on others when something isn't absolutely right. Some make enemies through their tendency to criticize, and refuse to appreciate or validate the talents or achievements of others. Others display some truly weird behavior.

Virgo Vivienne couldn't rest unless her house was picture-perfect. It wasn't a home that one could live in, but a showcase, and a demonstration of what a perfect home and a perfect world should be like. She could hardly bring herself to cook anything in her gleaming modern kitchen for fear of splashing and staining a pan. When her poor, long-suffering husband, Gary, painted their living room for the umpteenth time and left a tiny mark near the baseboard, she went on and on at him until he fixed it—almost demanding that he repaint the whole room. Gary is now retired, and the golf course has become his second home.

Virgo Monica worked at a health club and also wrote for a health magazine from time to time. She didn't look crazy, but I realized that she was nutty as a fruitcake when she admitted to me that she couldn't sleep at night because she worried that the river would rise to twice its height and inundate her home. She didn't even live near the river. Perhaps she'd been swept away and drowned in a previous life? I should have suggested that she get herself regressed and find out, because it certainly made no sense in this life.

A Leo friend named Carrie told me the next story. Carrie works in the medical field, and as Virgos tend to be drawn to hospital work, it isn't surprising that Carrie has come across a number of them. Carrie says that Virgos are good workers who always try to do what is asked of them, but they sometimes struggle to pick up technical systems. So when someone like the average Leo comes along and finds the task easy, the struggling Virgo gets angry and overreacts.

CAREERS

The Virgo needs a creative outlet; thus, many become actors, dancers, choreographers, writers, illustrators, designers, or anything else in the arty and creative field. Some are great cooks, and many are drawn to the health field. Others love to serve the less fortunate, such as in alcohol or drug rehabilitation centers, and they are often so busy helping others that they sometimes forget to look after themselves. A few go into finance or work in large corporations, such as banking or oil companies, where they work hard and reach great heights, but neglect their families. Virgos are always on the run, looking at their watches and getting geared up for the next meeting.

VIRGO AT HOME

Most Virgos prefer friends to family life, or have a family but rarely see them. My Virgo friend Jim went to many functions and dinner parties as part of his job, but nobody ever set eyes on his wife. I guess that's why they stayed married. Other Virgos try their hand at a marriage or two, but the emotional effort needed to keep a relationship going on a day-to-day basis really is too much for them. Virgos love sex, and will happily invite a friend over for an evening of passion, but once their pal has gone home, they make themselves a hot drink and sink into a favorite chair to watch TV, and *that* may well be the best part of the night for them.

I knew one much-divorced Virgo man who lost his home in a divorce. He worked as a store manager, so he moved an air mattress, microwave, and television into the back of the store and lived there. He was quite happy there, because it was peaceful and he didn't have to pay rent or any household bills.

While we're on the subject of paying for things, it's always good to ensure that Virgos, like all earth signs, know who is going to pay for what before going into any kind of business arrangement. Even going out for a meal with them is tricky, because earth signs don't mind looking bad, so when you've finished the meal and it's time to pay, they sit back with their hands interlaced over their full tummies, with smiles on their lips and no intention of contributing.

BODY AND HEALTH

Traditional Virgo problem areas are the bowels and nervous complaints; this is borne out by reality, because they do suffer from irritable bowel syndrome, ulcerative colitis, Crohn's disease, and piles. Some Virgos are absolute hypochondriacs, while others have to concentrate on their health due to some long-term chronic ailment. Many of them sooth their nerves by being heavy smokers, while a small minority drink too much or use drugs. Diabetes is common for this sign.

VIRGO TRIVIA

- Virgos are happy to plod along with the same daily routine for years. They are stubborn and dislike variety and change.

- This sign prefers short city breaks to long beach holidays, and too much heat upsets them.

- Virgos are stingy, but if they do spend money, it is on property or other things that will last.

- This is the sign of the critic and proofreader, which is why so many of them are in publishing.

- If Virgo goes in for drinking or drugs, he makes a good job of it. Witness

Amy Winehouse, Charlie Sheen, and Michael Jackson.

- Virgos appreciate good things, and a Virgo lady may have suitors who buy her designer clothes and take her to the best of places. Others are just cultured, but in a down-to-earth way.

VIRGO CELEBRITIES

- ★ Beyoncé
- ★ Sean Connery
- ★ Cameron Diaz
- ★ Colin Firth
- ★ Richard Gere
- ★ Hugh Grant
- ★ Liz Greene
- ★ Prince Harry
- ★ Julio Iglesias
- ★ Michael Jackson

- ★ Stephen King
- ★ Sophia Loren
- ★ John McCain
- ★ Freddie Mercury
- ★ Philippa Middleton
- ★ Keanu Reeves
- ★ Claudia Schiffer
- ★ Charlie Sheen
- ★ Shania Twain
- ★ Amy Winehouse

CHAPTER FOURTEEN:

SUN SIGN LIBRA

SEPTEMBER 23 TO OCTOBER 22

Planet:	Venus
Symbol:	The Scales
Gender:	Masculine
Element:	Air
Quality:	Cardinal
Number:	Seven

I can resist anything but temptation.
   —Oscar Wilde, playwright / poet

LIBRA THINGS

Traditional astrology color	Green, pink
Actual preferred color	Blue, pink
Metal	Copper
Gem	Pink stones, such as rose quartz
Likes	Good food and wine
House	Anywhere spacious and tidy with a good kitchen
Vacation	Pretty places and lovely gardens
Girlfriend	A woman with a collection of weird underwear
Boyfriend	A man who loves frequent arguments

THE MYTH

Libra is associated with love, partnerships, marriage, harmony, togetherness, sweetness, and gentleness. Librans have a strong sense of justice, so they make good lawyers and arbitrators, agents, and people who bring others together for some useful purpose. They are indecisive, weak, unwilling to give an opinion, and they hate violence or noisy rows.

THE REALITY

Libra is a masculine sign, ruled by a feminine planet; however, it's also a cardinal air sign, which makes it able to take charge of situations and do things quickly, while at the same time standing back, debating, theorizing, and looking at everything from all sides. No wonder Libra drives itself and everyone around it nuts. Libran hearts can sometimes be in the right place, but they have a tendency to argue. And yet they are often very lucky, leading what seem to be charmed lives and living in considerable comfort. Some are hard workers, but in other cases, one wonders where their money comes from.

Librans are sophisticated, good company, and they are quite good listeners. They are attractive to look at and always well dressed. They can be knowledgeable, diplomatic, sympathetic, and able to fit in with any company. They are great fun for a night out or for a short vacation. I have it on good authority from several friends and clients that they are wonderful in bed. They love meals out, laughing, going to concerts and events, and they are good dancers. They can sing and play musical instruments. Some years ago, I had a very responsible job, and my second in command was a Libran girl named Kate; she was the absolute best. I couldn't have found anyone more responsible, loyal, hardworking, pleasant, and enjoyable to work with, and we had a good laugh every single day.

Having said all of the above, living with Librans can be a nightmare, because the two scales make them pleasant when they want to be, or moody and confrontational when they don't. They can imagine that you have insulted them when you have not; they can insist that you have cheated on them, when nothing is further from the truth, and then use their manufactured hurt to start yet another exhausting argument. They are rarely physically violent because they don't need to be; they get the reaction they want by means of their intellect and quick, nasty tongues. They never give in, even if the argument goes on for weeks on end, and they can't or won't see that the other person might be right. Some Librans can start a fight in an empty room. Some are sympathetic and kind on one occasion, and then rude and uncaring on another.

I've known one or two whose marriages broke up because they insisted on having everything done their way. The arguments exhausted the poor men to the point where they had no more strength left to fight. One found another wife, and the other emigrated to the other side of the planet to get away from his wife's mouth.

I remember seeing a Libran boss man who worked for him, and the poor guy was so unnerved by the tirade that he actually shook in his shoes. I made the effort to discover what the victim had done, and it turned out to be nothing at all. The Libran boss had just gotten out of the wrong side of the bed that day.

Despite all this, many Librans hate to dwell on things that are ugly, unpleasant, or hurtful, and they can forget their own past and live in the present—exactly the way that modern gurus tell us to do. If they don't like someone, Librans can hide their feelings and behave with tact, diplomacy, and humor.

LOOKS

All races and types of Librans are usually extremely good-looking, and some are absolutely stunning. Both sexes have nice smiles that are full of humor, and large, luminous eyes. They don't usually put on much weight, and they can still look good as they age. Some have square and heavy faces, sometimes with bushy eyebrows, but whatever their looks, Librans of both sexes are vain. These people are extremely clean and tidy, and they keep their clothes and shoes in good condition. Their wardrobes are stuffed with clothes and if they have to travel, they try to take everything with them. Cruises are ideal for Librans, as there is no restriction on the amount of luggage one can take along. Librans are often described as being refined and elegant, and they are the kind of people who you can take anywhere and relax in the knowledge that they will behave perfectly. But Simon Cowell and Sharon Osborne are also Librans!

LIBRAN WOMEN

I was watching the admirable Libran Judge Judy on television recently while she was trying to get a reaction out of a poor guy who was so paralyzed with fright that he could hardly speak. Astonishingly, the woman who was suing him jumped in on his behalf and said that he "had a problem with confrontation." Judge Judy replied that she *never* had a problem with confrontation! Librans have a powerful sense of justice and good, quick minds, and they love adversarial argument, which is why so many of them go into the law, politics, trades unions, or other areas of arbitration and negotiation.

Libran women like a nice home and some have children, but they aren't fond of housework, gardening, or child-minding, so they go out to work. Libran women are good-looking, and they finance their looks with a great job and by marrying well. They ensure that they maintain a designer wardrobe, a good beauty salon, tanning booths, seaweed wraps, special diets to keep the fat, flab, and cellulite at bay, and a good nail salon.

CAREERS

There are several typically Libran areas of operation. One is the whole law/politics/agency thing, and another is what I would call the creation of beauty, embracing hairdressing, beauty salon work, stage and film makeup, gardening, painting, and book illustration. Also sewing, crocheting, and knitting. Many work in the music business, and many sing and play instruments. I have known Libran choirmasters, trombonists, and banjo players.

Many are drawn to work in cafés or restaurants, where they are especially good with the customers. A Libran restaurant manager ensures that his good clients enjoy the best tables and service. Librans hear all the latest gossip, but they can be surprisingly good at keeping the things they overhear to themselves. Some are great cooks, but while they may spend time working out new dishes for a restaurant, the day-to-day work of a busy kitchen is not for them. Some are extremely artistic and work in an artistic or creative field, such as dress design or designing theater sets.

Graham's office always looked pristine, and if he passed by someone else's office and saw a desk covered in papers, he would make a sarcastic remark at best or even order the person to clean it up. He couldn't stand the sight of a mess. However, while the surfaces in Graham's office were clean and tidy, the cupboards and drawers were overflowing with paper that had been shoved in any old way. None of this mattered to Graham, though, because the appalling mess wasn't visible to the naked eye!

Sports aren't really at the top of the Libran list of hobbies—they don't usually play rough games or team games. Ballroom and traditional kinds of dance appeal to Librans because they love to have a partner, and they enjoy the glamour and sheer beauty involved in the ballroom scene. All the Librans I have known are very good dancers. Many are into music and singing, and many work in the world of music production. Librans are hip, up-to-date, and classy. If a Libran took up hip-hop music and rapping, he would be the best dressed and most poetic of them all. Libran Eminem is an example. Watch the film *8 Mile,* and you will hear his wonderful poetry and admire his style and acting talent.

Librans are quite good at do-it-yourself projects, and some do extensive work on their homes, which end up looking tasteful and welcoming. They rarely do this kind of work for a living, though. Some knit or crochet wonderful garments, and many make their own clothes, or actually work in the garment trade as designers. They can be very skilled. My Libran mother used to make clothes for the British Royal Family and top actors and celebrities of all kinds, as well as many ordinary people.

THE OTHER SCALE

Librans are noted for having two very different sides to their natures, and this certainly was the case with Jamie, who was a sweet and gentle guy who loved music, played several instruments, and owned a massive collection of much-loved CDs. Jamie and I became friends when I was still at school, and we remained pals until his untimely death from a heart attack. Like most Librans, he hated racism and injustice, and he was a patriot. Most people talk a good fight, but Jamie spent his life attached to the army in a mysterious way that had something to do with the secret service, so he put his life on the line for our country many times.

BODY AND HEALTH

Librans can suffer from diabetes or heart disease, due to eating too much rich food over a long period of time. Their throats are vulnerable and they get tonsillitis, colds, flu, and bronchitis, and I have known one or two who have had throat cancer. At the time of writing, Michael Douglas has just completed being treated for throat cancer. Some have serious problems with their lower backs. Many have sensitive skin, while some suffer from hay fever.

LIBRA TRIVIA

- Librans have a faultless sense of style, which they bring to their jobs and their homes.

- Librans don't like messes, and they literally sweep untidiness out of sight, but they also dislike throwing stuff away, so their wardrobes and cupboards are stuffed to the brim.

- If they like an article of clothing, Librans buy a dozen of it in every color.

- Librans rarely work alone, but they can live alone quite happily as long as they have plenty of interests, activities, and friends.

- Librans aren't into team games; they like one-on-one games, such as tennis or squash. While they may take up boxing or wrestling, they prefer watching these sports to participating in them.

LIBRA CELEBRITIES

- ★ Vladimir Putin
- ★ Sylvia Browne
- ★ Deepak Chopra
- ★ Simon Cowell
- ★ Matt Damon
- ★ Snoop Dog
- ★ Eminem
- ★ Kim Kardashian
- ★ Roger Moore
- ★ Clive Owen
- ★ Gwyneth Paltrow
- ★ Will Smith
- ★ Bruce Springsteen
- ★ Gwen Stefani
- ★ Margaret Thatcher
- ★ Jean-Claude Van Damme
- ★ Sigourney Weaver
- ★ Serena Williams
- ★ Kate Winslet
- ★ Catherine Zeta-Jones

CHAPTER FIFTEEN

SUN SIGN SCORPIO

OCTOBER 23 TO NOVEMBER 21

Planet:	Mars & Pluto
Symbol:	The Scorpion
Gender:	Feminine
Element:	Water
Quality:	Fixed
Number:	Eight

Astrology is a language. If you understand this language, the sky speaks to you.
—Dane Rudhyar, author / astrologer

SCORPIO THINGS

Traditional astrology color	All shades of red
Actual preferred color	All pinks and reds, blue, black
Metal	Iron
Gem	Any red stone, such as ruby, garnet, or jasper
Likes	Traveling
House	Large, but easy to manage
Vacation	Wide open spaces, deserts, mountains
Girlfriend	Combination of brains and a desire for frequent sex
Boyfriend	Someone with a great sense of humor

THE MYTH

Traditional astrology says that Scorpio is difficult, dangerous, hot-tempered, hot in bed, and frankly too much for anybody but another Scorpio to cope with. Cautious and secretive, these people supposedly know what's in everyone else's minds while keeping their own doings close to their chests. Scorpio is said to be drawn to the dark side of psychism and black magic, and can be seen cooking up spells in a cauldron any day of the week. Having a Scorpio parent is judged to be the curse of the century.

THE REALITY

In my experience, Scorpios love animals, and while some aren't keen on children, others love them dearly and become totally enamored with their grandchildren. Also, most Scorpios have a good sense of humor, so how's that for the myth being one thing and reality being another? Sure, this sign has some nasty sides to it, but the good sides tend to get forgotten. Worse still, the truly aggravating aspects of the Scorpio nature are never properly described.

This is a fixed water sign, which is a contradiction of terms because water needs to flow, so they have the hidden depths of a lake, but also the speed of a flowing river. Scorpios can be very thorough, studying the subjects that interest them in great depth and getting the qualifications that they need. Although they aren't naturally attuned to modern technology, they cope with it. They hate bookkeeping, though, and they soon find someone else to do it for them. Scorpios do things quickly, and they can be efficient and effective. They seem to believe that life is a race and that the prize goes to the quickest. They don't like others to be in control of them, but they can seek to control others, and they certainly like their own way. They are brilliant salespeople—they aren't above making things sound bigger and better than they really are, and sometimes they even believe their own propaganda!

If you want to understand where Scorpios are coming from, the answer is that they are coming straight from their last emotion. For instance, if they look forward to some event, they can be as overexcited as children about it, and then they often end up being disappointed by the event, as it could never match up to the kind of expectation that they'd given it. Conversely, if they are angry or upset about something, there is no half measure, as they quickly become enraged.

Scorpios need very calm and laid-back partners. If they marry the sensitive psychic type of person who picks up on the emotions of others and gets upset, the marriage can't last. Scorpios need to marry those who don't pick up on atmospheres or get frightened by someone else's bad mood. Scorpios are very moody. They can have a bad day at work, bring it home, pick a fight, and then give their partner the silent treatment that goes on for hours, days, weeks or even months, to the point where the Scorpio doesn't even know what set them off in the first place. Scorpio's main fear is boredom, and sometimes they create a fight or some other drama just to keep boredom at a distance. Some really need to book themselves into an anger management course. They know how to hurt, punish, and destroy others, and they can and often do kill off the relationships that they most need.

Scorpios get annoyed about things that only make sense to them. For instance, when Scorpio Teresa needed to replace her car, rather than buy a pretty car with a zippy engine, she bought an ugly, gray car with a diesel engine. It must have been like driving an old lady's walker.

THE STING IN THE TAIL

Some Scorpios can be extremely nasty, hurtful, and destructive. They can be dreadful to work for and appalling to live with. Their moods change and they lash out or punish others with stony silences for no reason that anyone can discern. Prisons are probably full of these nasty, violent, and psychotic Scorpios. They seek out vulnerable people, use them unmercifully, and hurt them. They can be the worst parents in the world, utterly destroying any sense of self-worth in their children. They don't hold back for politeness or consider the feelings and needs of others.

THE ANGELIC SIDE OF SCORPIO

Scorpios are extremely loyal, and if happily married, they stay very close to their families. Scorpio loyalty extends not only to their loved ones, but to their dentists, doctors, accountants, lawyers, clubs, groups of friends, and so on. They don't like change for the sake of it, so they keep to the same faces for as long as possible. They don't move houses or change locations very easily, either. I knew one Scorpio lady who was looking for love and found a potential partner, but he lived about fifty miles from her. He had created a lovely garden that he was reluctant to leave, but she just wouldn't move to be with him, so she dropped him and continued her search elsewhere.

Scorpios can also be surprisingly sacrificial, and they can keep this up year in and year out, often looking after elderly parents who aren't especially grateful or pleasant. This sign is surprisingly dutiful. They have very acute, quick minds and great intelligence, and they are supposed to be able to see through people, but this isn't born out in reality. Scorpios have a habit of putting those who they like on pedestals and blinding themselves to the reality of the person, then being very badly let down.

Scorpio Trevor worked for a very wealthy man and thought the world of him. Trevor's wife wasn't so sure about the wonderfulness of the boss or of his haughty, greedy family. Like most young people starting out in life, Trevor had a large mortgage, and just when his wife had left her job to have their first baby, Trevor's boss announced that he'd sold the business and that Trevor should start looking for another job. Trevor went to the boss's house and begged him to help him find another job, or at least give him a couple of weeks' money to see him through. The boss coldly told Trevor to leave. Trevor was amazed and very upset at this turn of events, but his more practical wife wasn't the least bit surprised.

SCORPIO POSSESSIVENESS

Scorpios have a reputation for possessiveness and jealousy, but this can manifest itself in peculiar ways. My friend Julia was married to a Scorpio named Victor. He didn't care when she talked to men and he never accused her of flirting with other men in the way that so many insecure men do. His possessiveness was subtler than that, as it was directed toward her working life. He absolutely detested the thought of her putting her considerable talents and energy out there for the benefit of someone else, so he did his best to prevent her from going to work. Eventually, Julia got so tired of fighting for the right to go to work that she started her own business and became a big success. Fortunately, this suited them both.

SIZZLING SCORPIO

A strong dose of Scorpio on a chart can give an aura of sexiness that may or may not really exist. This is often the case with actors who light up the screen, but who may or may not be especially sexy in their private lives. A dose of Scorpio on any chart can lend sexiness to an otherwise fairly boring person.

LOOKS

Scorpios are pleasant-looking with excellent bone structure, nice eyes, good hair, and a warm smile. Most are average height and some are tall, but it's also quite common for Scorpios to be tiny, and for the men to resemble jockeys. The small types of Scorpios don't eat much, so they remain slim throughout life. Most are physically strong and can lift amazingly heavy weights.

BODY AND HEALTH

Scorpio rules the reproductive organs, and it's true that Scorpio women have trouble with the uterus and ovaries, but so do a lot of other women. Many Scorpios have sensitive stomachs and suffer from indigestion, and most can't cope with spicy food. Some are very fussy eaters or even vegans. Many Scorpios suffer from lower back problems, but the main problem is the weak Scorpio heart. This sign above all others should eat properly, exercise, avoid smoking, and take it easy from time to time. Above all, they must find an outlet for their pent-up natures.

SCORPIO TRIVIA

- Scorpios can have a falling-out with neighbors or colleagues and then occupy the same space for the next half century without speaking to them.

- Many Scorpios dislike eating with others or in front of others.

- Scorpios are tightfisted toward others, but they can be very indulgent to themselves.

- Scorpios either drink excessively or drink practically no alcohol at all.

- Scorpios can make public scenes without becoming embarrassed, but they don't like others doing so.

- Too many children of Scorpio parents spend their nights rocking on the stairs while the Scorpios throw things and scream.

- Nothing energizes a Scorpio more than the thought of a trip. In years gone by, the symbol for Scorpio was the eagle, and this makes much more sense than a scorpion. Scorpios roam far and wide.

SCORPIO CELEBRITIES

- ★ Bryan Adams
- ★ Mahmoud Ahmadinejad
- ★ Boris Becker
- ★ Richard Burton
- ★ Hillary Clinton
- ★ Jamie Lee Curtis
- ★ Leonardo DiCaprio
- ★ Calista Flockhart
- ★ Jodie Foster
- ★ Bill Gates
- ★ Whoopi Goldberg
- ★ Goldie Hawn
- ★ Demi Moore
- ★ Chris Noth
- ★ Kelly Osbourne
- ★ Condoleezza Rice
- ★ Julia Roberts
- ★ Meg Ryan
- ★ Winona Ryder
- ★ Martin Scorsese

CHAPTER SIXTEEN:
SUN SIGN SAGITTARIUS

NOVEMBER 22 TO DECEMBER 21

Planet:	Jupiter
Symbol:	The Centaur
Gender:	Masculine
Element:	Fire
Quality:	Mutable
Number:	Nine

I don't believe in astrology; I'm a Sagittarius and we're skeptical.
    —Arthur C. Clarke, science fiction author / futurist

SAGITTARIUS THINGS

Traditional astrology color	Royal blue
Actual preferred color	Blue and beige combinations
Metal	Tin
Gem	Sapphire
Likes	Travel, novelty, foreign languages
House	Easy to lock up and safe to leave while away traveling
Vacation	Backpacking to weird and extreme places
Girlfriend	Someone who doesn't mind being dumped when she gets pregnant
Boyfriend	A traveler or gambler with a good sense of humor

THE MYTH

The standard descriptions suggest that Sagittarius is an explorer, roaming the world with his loyal dog and equipped with nothing but a small backpack of essentials. More sensibly, traditional astrology tells us that Sagittarians travel a lot, becoming involved with foreigners or foreign goods, and speaking several languages. They are interested in religion or spirituality, as well as further or higher education, and they make good teachers or lawyers. This is a mutable fire sign, so it implies transformation at the speed of light, and a love of change and variety.

THE REALITY

A lot of the Sagittarian myth actually makes sense, although some qualities match one Sagittarian and others match the next. The main theme with Sagittarians is they don't understand boundaries or how far they should go in any situation, as we will see in this chapter.

Something that isn't mentioned in astrology books is the ghastly Sagittarius childhood, which can range from deeply irritating to nightmarish. At best, the child's parents or guardians aren't much use to them, but at worst, they are selfish, cruel, and abusive. Sometimes a parent is into a rigid religious belief, or the parents enforce something severe, such as only allowing their children to eat uncooked, strictly vegan food. Many parents are just plain embarrassing. I remember one Sagittarian whose mother carried a bag containing cooking pots everywhere with her in case she suddenly needed them, presumably to cook a meal for herself in the middle of a city street!

These children are bright, often nice-looking, and they have a great sense of humor. In some cases, the painful childhood destroys them so much that they descend into drinking, drugs, and lawbreaking. Others use their ability to make people laugh by becoming successful comedians or actors. Some grow up unable to care about others and become prickly and argumentative, quick to take offense over nothing. Obviously, these are the extremes. Nevertheless, the best part of childhood for this sign can be leaving it behind. Sagittarians often travel in order to escape, search for adventure, or go on a spiritual journey. Some make a point of creating a particularly wonderful family for themselves, while others push for independence and total freedom from family obligations. Sagittarians seem to have a deep need to get in touch with the spiritual side of life, either via established religion or via the psychic sciences.

TRUE STORIES

These stories denote Sagittarian themes of emigration, languages, foreigners, and making an inward journey to find a personal belief. Each suffered losses and then found his own way to fulfillment. The legal connection is that of visas, passports, changes of citizenship, patriotism, and of having status and jobs forced upon them by law. All these people are well educated, although mainly self-taught. They all work or worked in jobs that take in a variety of tasks, and with lots of different people.

Sagittarian Roger's parents gave him away when he was two years old because a second child came along and his silly, selfish mother felt that she couldn't cope with two children. He never got over the hurt. In time, he became an electrician by day and a medium and healer in his spare time, meeting new people all the time, which is a typical Sagittarian lifestyle.

Italian Sagittarian Giuseppe's father moved a new woman into their home, so his wife divorced him. Italian laws in those days only recognized men's rights, so the father deliberately hurt his wife by taking custody of his sons and then dumping them in an orphanage many miles from where she and their baby daughter lived. Giuseppe grew up and became an electrician. He fell in love with an English girl named Carla, moved to England, and married her. He now works in a high-level job that involves travel, a variety of tasks, and meeting new people. He and Carla are happy. Giuseppe has also discovered his psychic side, and he reads Tarot cards.

CHARACTERISTICS

The big deal with this sign is its inability to understand the need for boundaries. Sagittarians seek freedom and changes of scene, so you won't get anywhere by trying to control them, or even smothering them with love. They need to come and go when they feel like it, and just be who they want to be. This doesn't mean they are looking for opportunities to cheat; it's just the way they are. Some are very faithful to their lovers, while others won't stay with the same person for more than two weeks at a time. They are great to chat with at a party and can be a good laugh, but when boredom sets in, they leave the party long before it winds to a close. Those who are absolutely committed to family life choose careers that give them variety and the opportunity to travel and meet new people.

I would term this an intellectual sign, because Sagittarians tend to think a lot and study subjects deeply. They have quick minds, but they are also immensely practical and capable. I once asked a very pretty, young Sagittarian editor friend if she was good at DIY, and she replied that she had practically rebuilt her house from the bottom up.

This sign is noted for its spontaneity and for its love of doing something different. When my husband, Jan, was single, he tested the theory by sending a strange message to a Sagittarian woman who was also single and who had just joined a department in his firm. Interestingly, he and the woman had never met. The message read: *Would you like to come to lunch and then go to a demonstration of fire-walking with me?* He said that she accepted the invitation with enthusiasm. I recently suggested an evening of ghost-hunting to a young Sagittarian friend, and she jumped at it.

Sagittarians can listen to those who they respect and they can sop up information quickly, so they do become very knowledgeable, but they can also believe that they are right when it isn't necessarily so. They can be pulled in two directions at once, wanting stability and adventure at the same time, so they do suffer from a certain amount of confusion.

CAREERS

Sagittarians make good broadcasters and filmmakers, because they can live a strong fantasy life and have a roomy inner world. This can also take them into work as ministers of religion. Most religions depend upon faith, and that works well for the Sagittarian. They can exaggerate, and that makes them difficult to do business with, as one never knows what's real and what isn't. They have a strong sense of justice that can take them into legal work or union negotiations, where they fight for the rights of the underdog. A Sagittarian's life is something like driving very fast along a mountain road that doesn't have enough of a wall to stop them from falling off the edge, and in some cases they may even end up in mental institutions. Sometimes this is a result of addiction to drinking or drugs, but this isn't a strong-minded sign, so it can just be a case of finding life too hard to cope with.

THE SAGITTARIAN FAULT LINE

Lovely as they often are, Sagittarians can also be a pain in the butt. At best, they put their feet in their mouths, saying the wrong thing at the wrong time. They can make jokes when it would be better not to. Some have very sharp tongues and will attack those who have no intention of doing them harm. Clever as they are, they are bad judges of character, so they can assume that people want to criticize or demean them when nothing is further from the truth. Their silly, great mouths are often twenty times larger than their brains, and this costs them real friendships, screwing up their chances of getting along with others in the workplace. They need to stop, count to ten, analyze things, and work out whether they should let their nasty side loose, or whether they will do themselves and others more good by keeping quiet. They are born with the blessing of good luck, but they can also get themselves into a mess by leaping before looking.

Amazingly for such a sunny-natured fire sign, they are stingy. They spend money like water on travel or on stuff for themselves, but they don't see it as any part of their business to help others. They are takers rather than givers. If a Sagittarian comes to your house for tea, they can easily move in, but the good news is that they don't stay anywhere for long, so they will move out again fairly quickly, at which point it's worth getting the locks changed!

One Sagittarian I knew recovered from alcoholism but then became hooked on a strange form of weirdly destructive behavior. He would lose his temper and throw expensive electronic typewriters, photocopiers, and other heavy equipment down the stairs of his office building. Fortunately, he owned the business!

SAGITTARIUS AND SEX

Those who are into sex tell me that there isn't anything a Sagittarian won't do. They can be bisexual, trisexual, and everything in between. A friend of mine once had a very cheerful, bright, good-looking Sagittarian pal named Lucas who was in his mid-twenties, bisexual, and the father of six children by six different women. Needless to say, Lucas never parted with one penny in child support for any of his offspring!

LOOKS

Most Sagittarians have smiley eyes and a lovely smile. Some have a long chin or even a lantern jaw, although this becomes less obvious as they age and put on weight. Their bodies are medium to tall and somewhat out of proportion, either with large top halves and slim hips, or small tops and heavy hips and legs.

BODY AND HEALTH

Tradition tells us that the Sagittarian weak spots are the hips and thighs, but some suffer from hypochondria, so they can dream up (and even come down with) an amazing array of ailments.

SAGITTARIUS TRIVIA

- Sagittarians are great company at a party or when working at a festival for a few days, but they are hard to live with on a long-term basis.

- Sagittarius is the most eccentric sign of the zodiac.

- Despite the fact that Sagittarians are supposed to be fond of horses, most don't like horses or large animals because they prefer small animals, especially dogs.

- When Sagittarians are angry, they get nasty and can even be cruel to children.

- My husband calls Sagittarians Mr. and Mrs. Quickfix, because they are great at coming up with swift solutions to urgent problems.

SAGITTARIUS CELEBRITIES

- ★ Christina Aguilera
- ★ Woody Allen
- ★ Kim Basinger
- ★ Ludwig van Beethoven
- ★ Ted Bundy
- ★ Ann Dunham (Barack Obama's mother)
- ★ Jane Fonda
- ★ Jake Gyllenhaal
- ★ Jimi Hendrix
- ★ Jay-Z
- ★ Brad Pitt
- ★ Keith Richards
- ★ Frank Sinatra
- ★ Britney Spears
- ★ Steven Spielberg
- ★ Joseph Stalin
- ★ Kiefer Sutherland
- ★ Taylor Swift
- ★ Tina Turner

CHAPTER SEVENTEEN:

SUN SIGN CAPRICORN

DECEMBER 22 TO JANUARY 20

Planet:	Saturn
Symbol:	The Goat
Gender:	Feminine
Element:	Earth
Quality:	Cardinal
Number:	Ten

When a Capricorn falls in love, he is sincere. Unfortunately, this doesn't usually happen during his lifetime.

—Sasha Fenton, professional astrologer / author

CAPRICORN THINGS

Traditional astrology color	Brown, gray
Actual preferred color	Brown, gray, dark red, mustard, orange
Metal	Lead
Gem	Topaz, tiger's eye, garnet
Likes	Status symbols, Porsches
House	Large, with a good entertainment system
Vacation	A luxury cruise with high-class passengers
Girlfriend	A classy, good-looking woman
Boyfriend	Anyone with money

THE MYTH

Astrology books tell us that Capricorns are hardworking, ambitious, thorough, practical, dependable, sensible, respectable, dour, silent, reclusive, inclined to be negative, and often religious. Some astrology books concede that Capricorns have a dry sense of humor. Astrologers tell us that Capricorns are stingy and that many of them are also snobbish.

THE REALITY

The people of this sign are classy and intelligent, and they don't like anything that is low-brow or not trendy. They know that nastiness exists, but they don't want to see, hear, or deal with any of it.

Capricorns are ambitious, and if there is a hill to climb, just like the mountain goat that's their symbol, they will clamber upward. Astrologers sometimes accuse Capricorns of being overambitious or too keen on making money, and there is some truth in this. Most are hardworking, reliable and extremely responsible folk. If their family needs money, they will work themselves into the ground to provide it. My feeling is that they hate to see themselves as lazy or time-wasters, and this may have come from the expectations of their parents and teachers when they were young, so that they've been programmed to keep running, like a hamster on a wheel.

Capricorns really love their homes and family life, and they are good to their parents. Capricorns can be pleasant as friends, but their real love is reserved for their relatives, especially the older generation. Capricorns work well, but they hate to be rushed, and they will also encourage others to do well.

Some Capricorns are surprisingly unconventional, because the deeply unconventional signs of Aquarius and Sagittarius bracket this sign, and it's likely that these people will have the planets that lie close to the Sun (Mercury and Venus) in one of these signs. Even if they are unconventional, the urge to move upward still exists, so those who get into the world of mind, body, and spirit soon find their way onto the most prestigious committees. Whatever their lifestyle, Capricorns are snobbish, which is a trait that they share with several other signs.

Although the image is of the Dickensian clerk, sitting at his old scarred desk, pouring over some massive journal, Capricorns prefer a job with a sales component to it. They are quite restless and love to travel, meeting clients and seeing the world. The world of publishing is absolutely full of Capricorns, because the combination of extremely detailed work, the sales component, and the aura of classiness that goes with the job.

You won't see this in any astrology book, but Capricorns love to travel—as backpacking students, old-folks who take cruises around the world, and everything else between. They love to get away and see the world, and while most prefer comfort, they can put up with camping and rough conditions if they have to.

CAPRICORN WOMEN

These women are ambitious, and while some make it for themselves, many link themselves to powerful, wealthy, and important men. Sometimes they have to wait a long time for their chosen man to come around to the idea of marriage, but this is a notably patient sign. Consider Kate Middleton, the new Duchess of Cambridge, who waited eight years for her prince to ask for her hand. Once safely married, Capricorn women have a child or two, but they also have a career or a business of their own. If her man is accustomed to spending his money very freely, the Capricorn wife curbs this tendency almost before the ink dries on the marriage certificate. Those who don't marry may link themselves with powerful and important men and then live in the vain hope of an eventual marriage proposal.

Despite their outward success—status symbols, nice cars, nice homes, and so on—Capricorn women lack confidence, and they can be worriers to the point of neurosis, partly because they don't trust their own judgment.

Things that wouldn't bother others for a moment loom large in their minds, and if they inadvertently make a mistake, they beat themselves up badly. As far as partnerships are concerned, a single Capricorn woman might play the field for a while, or she may not run around much. But once she finds her mate she is utterly faithful.

Capricorn is a cardinal sign, so when things don't work out, Capricorn cuts its losses, goes back to square one, and rebuilds. Being over thirty, Geraldine was becoming worried about finding a husband, so when a supposedly wealthy American named Paul came along, she jumped at the opportunity. Paul was divorced with two small daughters who lived with his ex-wife, so he was free to marry. After a whirlwind courtship, Paul announced that he needed a bit of financial help in the short term. Geraldine saw this as an investment in a glittering future, so she sold her modest London house and gave Paul the money. Three days into the marriage, Paul suddenly turned nasty and beat Geraldine badly. She wisely left the hotel without even packing, took a taxi to the airport, got a flight home, and started divorce proceedings. She moved back in with her mother for a couple of years, worked hard to get back on her feet, and put the whole incident behind her.

THE CAPRICORN MAN

I have absolute proof that some Capricorn men really love their families and are totally faithful to their partners, because my Capricorn stepfather was a good husband and a good stepfather, and he was thoughtful to his own aged parents and other relatives. However, many Capricorn men are seriously unfaithful. Here are some true stories:

There is a famous Capricorn athlete who had a wonderful, tiny, blond trophy wife, with whom no fashionista could compete. Yet despite the model of perfection waiting for him at home, the moment the athlete was away, he sought out one prostitute after another for companionship. His attitude was probably that these women were a form of relief that had nothing to do with his love for his wife and family. The wife didn't buy this, especially as it turned out that a couple of these extracurricular women had given birth to children.

Jennie had been seeing Richard for years. He wasn't married, but he lived with another woman. Naturally, Jennie sincerely believed that Richard would eventually leave the other woman and marry her. Then a series of family deaths and disasters overcame poor Jennie, and when she needed the love and comfort of the man who she'd loved for so long, he was nowhere to be found.

LOOKS

Capricorn ladies are good-looking, with the kind of chiseled features that age into increasing loveliness, and many of them have wonderfully rich, long, shiny hair. In the case of an African-American such as Michelle Obama, her beauty is captured in her pleasant looks, her style, and her superb physique. Men are of average height and can range in looks from ordinary to rather handsome. Some, like Elvis Presley, have a wonderful smile and great charisma.

Unless they are the unconventional type, most wear expensive, conservative clothes in black, gray, and dark brown, but some Capricorns insist on setting these off with vile tones of mustard, slime green, and orange. Capricorn women sport the "right" handbag—preferably something that has to be ordered several months in advance and that costs more than a fortune.

BODY AND HEALTH

Capricorn is known to be a long-lived sign, and these people are usually strong and healthy, continuing to work and pursue sports and hobbies well into old age. However, some have chronic ailments, such as asthma, skin problems, and rheumatism. Deafness is also something that afflicts many Capricorns, especially as they age.

CAPRICORN TRIVIA

- Capricorns believe in the old adage that if you look after the cents, the dollars will look after themselves.

- Some Capricorns are very quiet, especially if they are hard of hearing. Others are like talking machines that can't turn themselves off.

- Capricorns often work in jobs with a strong selling component.

- Capricorns can suffer from problems with their shins and knees, including a condition known as "housemaid's knee."

- This sign is ambitious and hardworking, and it also wants other members of the family to do well so it will do all it can to facilitate this.

- Women of this sign frequently have very nice hair, and even men keep their hair looking good throughout life.

- Capricorns look ordinary when young, but they age well and don't tend to become fat.

CAPRICORN CELEBRITIES

★ Muhammad Ali
★ Orlando Bloom
★ Nicolas Cage
★ Jim Carrey
★ Kate Middleton, Duchess of Cambridge
★ Kevin Costner
★ Gérard Depardieu
★ Mel Gibson
★ Cary Grant
★ Anthony Hopkins
★ Martin Luther King, Jr.
★ Jude Law
★ Marilyn Manson
★ Sienna Miller
★ Kate Moss
★ Michelle Obama
★ Michael Schumacher
★ Jon Voight
★ Denzel Washington
★ Tiger Woods

CHAPTER EIGHTEEN

SUN SIGN AQUARIUS

JANUARY 21 TO FEBRUARY 18

Planet:	Saturn & Uranus
Symbol:	The Water Carrier
Gender:	Masculine
Element:	Air
Quality:	Fixed
Number:	Eleven

We need not feel ashamed of flirting with the zodiac. The zodiac is well worth flirting with.

 —D. H. Lawrence, novelist / playwright

AQUARIUS THINGS

Traditional astrology color	Neon colors
Actual preferred color	Darkish shades of blue and purple
Metal	Uranium
Gem	Aquamarine
Likes	Any off-the-wall interest, music
House	Large, with plenty of room for gadgets, hobbies, and clutter
Vacation	Somewhere comfortable but not too crowded
Girlfriend	A slim woman who is into astrology and sex, and can act as secretary and backup memory
Boyfriend	Someone who travels for business so he isn't always hanging around and being boring

THE MYTH

Astrology books present a real problem where this sign is concerned, because they describe Aquarians as unconventional, eccentric, but logical, intelligent, and sensible; friendly, but also cool and detached. They are said to be inventive, original, and a catalyst for change, while also being fixed, determined, obstinate, and disinclined to change. People of this sign are said to take up causes, stand on soapboxes, and work for the benefit of humanity, but they are also stingy, self-absorbed, and disinclined to help others. My aged astrology books say that Aquarius was the sign of revolution, which leads to immovable, totalitarian governments. The myth is so polarized with opposites that it's hard to make any sense of it.

THE REALITY

An Aquarian friend who doesn't actually believe in astrology gave me the best description of the sign that I have ever heard. She said that there couldn't be anything in astrology, because her family is full of Aquarians and that each one was very different from all the others. She's right: not about astrology, but about Aquarians. Each Aquarian *is* totally different from every other Aquarian, and also different from everyone else on earth, which is why this sign is so tricky to categorize. Many Aquarians *are* unconventional and many make a point of looking different. In the words of an astrologer friend of mine named Sam, "You can always tell an Aquarian, because they come in for a reading dressed poorly."

I've known one who wore full Native American garb every day, despite working in a perfectly ordinary office job, while another went barefoot all day long, despite the cold weather and the fact that she looked inappropriate. On the other hand, I've known Aquarians of both sexes who are extremely well dressed.

INDEPENDENCE

Something that all Aquarians share is an independent mind and strong views. For instance, half are so deeply into astrology that they choose to work in the field, while the other half dismiss it without actually knowing anything about it. The following stories bear out the Aquarian need for the freedom that comes from self-employment.

Danielle worked as the maintenance manager in an office complex, and at one point she had to organize a crew of workers to renovate part of the building. This involved hiring a dozen self-employed tradesmen, such as builders, carpenters, electricians, plumbers, and so on. Being interested in astrology, she asked each one what sign they were; to her amazement, eleven of the twelve were Aquarians.

Some years ago, I happened to read a retired cat burglar's autobiography, and at one point in the book he mentioned astrology, saying with absolute certainty that it's completely bogus. He then said that there was one odd thing that he couldn't understand—namely, that he was an Aquarian and so were all his burglar friends!

LIVING AT A DISTANCE

Aquarians care deeply about a whole variety of things, as long as they are at a distance. Astrology committees are full of Aquarians, as are local government committees and other sources of good works. Many Aquarians work in education and are passionate about the needs of children, while others fight hard for the rights of animals. However, they can be detached to the point of blindness when it comes to their nearest and dearest. I remember one Aquarian woman whose child walked around in an outfit that he had outgrown that was so tight under his feet that the poor kid couldn't straighten his legs! Many Aquarians avoid having children at all.

AQUARIAN GENEROSITY

Aquarians are generous with their knowledge and their time, and they don't feel threatened by someone else making something of themselves. They are natural teachers, who are often catalysts who help others get on in life. When I was in my twenties, an Aquarian friend helped me get the education I had missed out on at school, and later, an Aquarian editor helped me get started and gave me every possible encouragement. I once asked both of these lovely people why they had been so helpful, and they said they loved to foster talent and hated to see it go to waste. Very few members of other signs are as generous and kind as Aquarians.

Some are tightfisted in silly ways, complaining about the cost of a postage stamp and so on. A friend named Polly was once married to an Aquarian named John, and one day Polly ran out of shampoo, so she helped herself to a couple of squeezes from John's bottle. He went absolutely ballistic and started a draining, three-day argument over it. On the other hand, my Aquarian husband would give me the clothes off his back. As I said, this is a sign of absolutes.

AQUARIUS AND BOOKS

If there is one thing that absolutely every Aquarian shares, it's a thirst for knowledge and a love of books. Most have so many books in their house that the floors are in danger of collapsing. Some fill their massive book collections with piles of newspapers, magazines, flyers, and bits of paper, none of which they can be persuaded to throw out. Modern technology, the Internet and smart phones are made for Aquarians. They need information at their fingertips at all times.

AQUARIUS AND POLITICS

Aquarians can do surprisingly unexpected things. Aquarian President Ronald Reagan managed to get the Soviet Union to give up the arms race. Apparently President Reagan and Prime Minister Margaret Thatcher liked each other so much that the press began to wonder whether the two geriatrics were having an affair.

With a few exceptions, most Aquarians merely rant about politics and are sure that they could do it all so much better, but they are normally too naive and lacking in street smarts to cope with the reality of the political scene.

TRUE STORIES

This is about the bizarre things that could only happen to an Aquarian. In this case, I'm not disguising the person or the circumstances, because this story is about my husband, who doesn't mind that I talk about him. Jan was born and raised in what was then Northern Rhodesia, which is now Zambia, in Southern Africa. Being a naturally intelligent, curious (and totally naive) child and an animal lover, he caught and kept snakes for a hobby, and whenever he got the chance, he played with other wild animals. This led to some serious injuries, including a three-month stint in a hospital fighting to keep his fingers and his life after an understandably irritated burrowing viper snake took a couple of bites out of him.

Many years later, he landed in a hospital when, after climbing out of a very hot bath, he fainted and hurt himself on the bathroom tiles as he fell. After a long wait, a bored and fatigued young hospital doctor came to take his medical history, and he yawningly asked whether Jan had spent any time in the hospital. Jan started with the usual "tonsils at the age of twenty" and then moved on to name bilharzia (twice). The doctor looked up momentarily from his clipboard. Then Jan mentioned the snakebite episode, and the doctor suddenly woke up and examined the mangled finger that Jan was cheerfully waving at him. After checking out the finger and hearing its story, the doctor then pointed to lines of stitch marks on Jan's forearms and asked about them. "Oh, they're just claw marks from a young leopard," drawled Jan. "Wow," said the doctor, "the last time I saw wounds like that was when I treated a circus performer!"

THE FAMOUS AQUARIAN "FORGETTERY"

An Aquarian will be your best friend, but when someone else comes along that looks more interesting, they may move on and forget your existence. They have such a funny attitude to long-term loyalty that they can even forget their own parents and children. However, in the short term, they can be wonderful friends. Having said that, my Aquarian friend moved away from the area where we both lived over two decades ago and I haven't seen her since, but we write to each other regularly, again illustrating the bizarre polarity of opposites that this sign encompasses.

LOOKS

Aquarians come in two quite opposite shapes and sizes, one being small and plump with round faces, nice eyes, and hair. Women of this type are often very pretty. The other type is tall and bony with long faces, high foreheads, and sometimes rather protruding ears, while some have fine, flyaway hair. These Aquarians can suffer from dry skin on their hands and faces. The hands look old, even when the person is still young, as they are quite lined and the knuckles are prominent.

BODY AND HEALTH

Astrology books tell us that Aquarian weak spots are the ankles and the Achilles tendon. Aquarian Arthur broke an ankle when he was young, while Aquarian James limped throughout his life after being hit by shrapnel in the ankle during World War II. Furthermore, my husband has sprained both ankles a number of times, and broken one ankle while playing squash. Having said that, most Aquarians actually suffer from back pain, deafness, skin problems, and memory loss. Aquarians are either tall or short, and rather heavy, and both these scenarios put a strain on their backs. One Aquarian I know has six sacral vertebrae instead of the normal five. Saturn is one of Aquarius's rulers, and it rules deafness. Memory loss is hard to spot in an Aquarian, because they can remember everything about Ancient Egypt or the intricacies of some weird sport or game, but none can remember to mail a letter or buy a loaf of bread, so when dementia strikes, there often isn't much noticeable change.

AQUARIUS TRIVIA

- Aquarians are possessive, although not usually unreasonably jealous.

- Most are friendly and want to be liked, but some are so self-important that they walk through rooms with their noses in the air.

- Aquarians seem laid-back, but the males of the species are easily irritated and many have hot tempers. Coupled with their sharp tongues, you can see why most of them go through several divorces.

- This sign often looks vague due to the lack of expression on the Aquarian face, but most are intelligent.

- Most consider themselves articulate, but speak very slowly.

- Most are happy to listen to what you have to say, but with minds completely closed to everything but their own points of view.

- Aquarians don't like change for its own sake, but the planet that rules the sign brings sudden unexpected change and even chaos at times.

AND FINALLY . . .

In the words of my husband, he takes all critical remarks about Aquarian bizarreness as compliments!

AQUARIUS CELEBRITIES

- ★ Jennifer Aniston
- ★ Sheryl Crowe
- ★ Geena Davis
- ★ Ellen DeGeneres
- ★ Matt Dillon
- ★ Paris Hilton
- ★ Alicia Keys
- ★ Paul Newman
- ★ Kim Novak
- ★ Yoko Ono

- ★ Sarah Palin
- ★ Lisa Marie Presley
- ★ Ronald Reagan
- ★ Axl Rose
- ★ Nicolas Sarkozy
- ★ Justin Timberlake
- ★ John Travolta
- ★ Robbie Williams
- ★ Oprah Winfrey

CHAPTER NINETEEN:
SUN SIGN PISCES

FEBRUARY 19 TO MARCH 20

Planet:	Jupiter & Neptune
Symbol:	The Fishes
Gender:	Feminine
Element:	Water
Quality:	Mutable
Number:	Twelve

Astrology is just a finger pointing at reality.
   —Steven Forrest, evolutionary astrologer

PISCES THINGS

Traditional astrology color	Sea blue
Actual preferred color	Blues, greens
Metal	Tin
Gem	Turquoise
Likes	Séances, the sea, travel
House	Must have a room for meditation and the owner's therapy work
Vacation	A tropical island
Girlfriend	Someone with a life of her own who doesn't want a permanent partner
Boyfriend	Someone to carry bags, organize outings, buy tickets, and pay for everything

THE MYTH

Traditional astrology tells us that Pisces is a gentle, mystical sign that belongs to people whose heads are so far in the clouds that they can't come to grips with anything practical. They are into religion, spirituality, mediumship, and witchcraft of all kinds. They can't handle money or understand business, so they float around in a haze while spending their lives searching for beauty. They comfort themselves with drinking, drugs, and other escapist pleasures.

THE REALITY

Pisceans are far from being weak or stupid, and they are perfectly capable of making a living for themselves and their families. They always look like they are broke, but they find plenty of money when it comes to something they want. There is often a method to their madness, and some of them are surprisingly hard and selfish, although others truly are kind and thoughtful. Most adore their children and often keep them close by long after they've grown up. If their grandchildren need a home, Pisceans will happily take them in. Their children will sometimes think they are easily taken advantage of, so Pisces folk need to control their urge to sacrifice too much for their loved ones. If their children and grandchildren have kind hearts and good natures, everything works out well.

I've noticed that there is always an element of chaos somewhere in the life of a Pisces, so if they are successful at their work, their family life is a mess, or if their family life is fine and they are managing to cope at work, their finances are in meltdown. They seem to live on the brink of disaster, and yet they don't fall into the abyss and actually end up living nice lives and doing pretty much what they feel like doing.

THE PISCES CHILDHOOD

Pisces boys are often artistic and gentle, and they frequently don't measure up to what many parents want,. Many Pisces children are psychic and spiritual. Some play with spirit children, while others are convinced that they've lived before. This is unnerving enough for parents, but it's often part of the Piscean karma to be born into a family that's deeply into some rigid religion, so to the eyes of the parents, their child is scary and in need of exorcism. Another twist to this tale is of children born into a nonreligious family, but who confuse everyone by becoming religious later.

Many spend long periods in the hospital, or sick in bed, thereby developing their inner worlds of imagination, creativity, and spirituality. If hospitalized, the enforced separation and the abnormality of the children's lives damage and perhaps destroy the bond that should exist between parents and children. Teenagers might get into trouble and spend a year or so in some kind of correctional facility.

Even if a child's home life is great, school might be a nightmare, so the best thing a Piscean can do is to grow up quickly. Pisces people instinctively feel this, so many marry and start to have children when they are very young, probably due to an inner urge to have someone to love who will love them in return. Many adore animals, and animals certainly love them back. Some remain faithful to their partners for life, but some have affairs or split up and make other relationships. A surprising number of them end up living alone.

THE PISCEAN BRAIN

Many Pisceans are left-handed, suggesting that their spatial, artistic right brains are stronger than the logical left-brain sides, and dyslexia is linked to left-handedness. Some are word-blind but find numbers easy, and others are the other way around. Many can't use computers, never learn to drive a car, or are even epileptic. Unless there's a lot of air in their charts, as in the case of actor Michael Caine, they are halting public speakers. Add their quiet voices, gentle manners, slow movements, and halting speech to the vague look that many of them have and you could easily make the mistake of thinking Pisceans are not smart, but you do so at your peril, as they are extremely shrewd. They know how to undermine and hurt others, to get the better of them, to have their cake and eat it, too, and to be the real winners of the zodiac.

CAREERS

Pisces people are attracted to any work that benefits others, such as jobs in hospitals, charities, social work, and childcare. They make wonderful salespeople, because they can tap into people's deepest desires and sell them a dream. Their visualization skills lead to dress design, pattern cutting, drawing blueprints, and working as engineers, while some buy and sell metal. Many serve others by cooking, waiting tables, or putting on events. A good number go into politics.

THE MANY OTHER SIDES OF THE COIN

Despite all its apparent softness, Pisces is not a soft sign, and these folk can survive almost anything. Faced with tough situations, many will drift away, leaving partners and children in their wake and soon finding replacements. Some take to drinking as a form of escape.

Like all water signs, Pisceans are moody and sometimes unpleasant. While they all appear friendly and very kindhearted, some are genuine while others aren't. I suspect that only another Pisces can tell which is which. Both sexes are moody and changeable. The lowest types are selfish, spiteful, and surprisingly competitive. They like to be seen as helpful people who do good works, but this can sometimes be an act that hides selfishness.

PISCES MOODINESS—OR THE PULL OF THE TIDES

I once had a Piscean friend named Daphne who was pleasant, humorous, and popular. When invited to a party, she would ask me to come along, and I would really look forward to it. A half hour after arriving (usually when I'd found someone nice to chat with), the tide would turn and Daphne would become angry and want to go home. She would be so loud and insistent that the only thing to do was to get into a cab and call it a day. After experiencing this a couple of times, I refused to go anywhere with Daphne.

PISCES THRIFT

Some Pisceans are reasonably generous to others, but reluctant to spend money on themselves, and some wear clothing that is so worn out that it qualifies as ragged. Some are perfectly reasonable to themselves but weird toward others, as in this true story:

Patrick was friendly with his ex-wife, and he liked to visit her from time to time. While he was at her house, he would send her on a quest for something, and when she was out of sight, he'd raid her fridge. Sometimes there was only enough time for him to scrape half a shelf into his bag, but on a lucky day when he could keep his ex busy for a longer period of time, he got a better haul. If his luck was exceptional, Patrick would visit when his ex was expecting company so that the quality of his takings would be at its best.

LOOKS

Both sexes are often nice-looking and frequently stunning when young. They have gentle, pleasant, open features and a lovely smile. They are slim, elegant, and great dancers. Some even know how to dress well. Sadly, later in life, the men get fat and resemble hamsters, while the women can develop puttylike features and gain weight, especially if they are drinkers.

BODY AND HEALTH

Piscean childhood ailments can be dreadful, and many suffer from chronic health problems, such as asthma, emphysema, or epilepsy. However, they often manage to overcome these things and live a normal life, and if they keep away from alcohol, they could probably live forever. The weak spots are supposedly the feet, but they suffer with their lungs, lymph system, and nerves. They can get peculiar allergies and skin problems.

PISCES TRIVIA

- Don't ever ask a Piscean to draw a map or even make a list of sensible directions. They think their directions are perfect, but everyone who tries to follow them gets hopelessly lost.

- If you are going to any event organized by a Pisces, be ready for anything.

- Pisceans can be wonderful cooks, but they don't actually get around to doing it very often.

- Pisceans are sensitive and psychic, and they can pick up vibes when walking into a new venue or when meeting new people.

- Sometimes Pisceans find themselves absorbing the feelings of others and becoming sad, happy, or angry when the sadness, joy, or anger really belongs to the person who is around them.

PISCES CELEBRITIES

★ Justine Bieber
★ Michael Caine
★ Johnny Cash
★ Chelsea Clinton
★ Glenn Close
★ Daniel Craig
★ Mikhail Gorbachev
★ Ted Kennedy
★ Liza Minnelli

★ Chuck Norris
★ Alan Rickman
★ Rihanna
★ Kurt Russell
★ Seal
★ Sharon Stone
★ Ivana Trump
★ Rachel Weisz
★ Bruce Willis

CONCLUSION:
BEYOND THE SUN SIGN

That's the inside story of how our Sun signs influence us. But it's just one of a number of influences on a horoscope. For instance, the way that the time and place of birth connects with a particular point along the zodiac gives you your Rising sign, and this reflects your early experiences of life—the way that your parents, siblings, schoolmates, other adults, and the kind of society that you grew up in worked to condition your outer manners and behavior. Your Moon sign explains your inner needs and feelings, the way you act when downhearted and ill, your habits and fallback position, and even the way you behave when in love. There are other planets that show mental agility, the things you value and love, the way you assert yourself, your good luck and chances to expand your horizons, your bad luck and limitations, and the influence of the times that you live through. All these items and more fall into positions called *houses* that show the way that each of these energies is directed.

Some people have charts that scream *health problems* to an astrologer; other charts indicate perpetual luck with money, while some show fortune in relationships but bad luck in friendship. Still others foretell wonderful friendships and huge success in life, but repeated disappointments in love. All these things and much more will only show up in a full horoscope chart. However, the Sun sign is still an exceedingly powerful influence.

My first introduction to astrology was a small chapter in an old fortune-telling book. The first words there told me that my nature was one of leadership, independence, and creativity, and that others would have good reason to trust me in business. I wouldn't disagree with any of that. It also said I could be snobbish, critical, and selective about whom I choose as friends. I wouldn't disagree with that, either.

Don't throw this book away after reading it—keep it on your bookshelf. When others behave in ways you can't understand, you may wonder what the inside story is to their actions. When that happens, look back over the book and you'll begin to understand their behavior by their Sun sign, and at the very least you'll have a good chuckle about it.

Good luck,
Sasha